Planned Life Assurance

MARTIN PATERSON

LONDON
BUSINESS BOOKS LIMITED

First published 1966
Second Edition 1969

SBN 220 99228 2

This book has been set in 12 on 13 pt. Bembo: made and printed in Great Britain by Cox and Wyman Limited, Reading, for the publishers, Business Books Limited (registered office: 180 Fleet Street, London, E.C.4), publishing offices: Mercury House, Waterloo Road, London, S.E.1

MADE AND PRINTED IN GREAT BRITAIN

Planned Life Assurance

Contents

Section III—Primarily for retirement and old age

PART FOUR—GENERAL

PART FIVE—FOR THE EMPLOYER

Preface

THIS BOOK has been written, not for the normal student of life assurance nor for the life assurance salesman, but primarily for the benefit of businessmen and professional people. It is hoped that it will prove of particular interest to those people who, whilst working outside the insurance industry, frequently have occasion to advise their clients or employees on life assurance matters. For this reason the subject is treated at a practical level and in a way which it is hoped will be helpful to those who buy life assurance rather than sell it.

March, 1966 M. P.

Preface to Second Edition

THE BOOK has been extensively revised following the 1968 Finance Act which made important changes in the treatment for tax and estate duty of life policies. The opportunity has been taken to describe new trends in life assurance and to illustrate some of the more important new contracts introduced to the market since the first edition was published in 1966.

February, 1969 M. P.

Acknowledgments

I WOULD like to express my gratitude to all those who have helped me to prepare the first and second editions of this book. I am particularly indebted to J. N. Crisfield for checking the draft chapters of the first edition: to C. J. Rye, F.C.I.I. for his close collaboration in the preparation of most of the examples in Part Three and to F. E. King, V.R.D., F.I.A. for checking these: to Equity and Law Life Assurance Society Ltd, for allowing me to draw freely on their published notes on the Finance Act, 1968, in connection with the revision of Chapters 3 and 4; to L. G. Hall, F.I.A. for the benefit of his expert advice on the investment of life funds and to the Life Offices Association for providing me with up-to-date statistical information.

I would also like to thank warmly my colleagues for the information they have helped to gather, for the ideas they have contributed and for their valuable advice and criticism.

Part One

INTRODUCTORY

I

Introduction

AN APPRECIATION of the scope and value of life assurance is assisted if two things are firmly understood. One is that the *object* of life assurance is to provide cover against death. This may be self-evident but it is often overlooked by those seeking a profitable outlet for their savings and comparing life assurance with other investment opportunities. The second is that all life assurance, other than temporary contracts, contains an element of investment, even when payment of the benefit is wholly dependent on death. To see this, it is only necessary to remember that as everyone must eventually die, insurance against death carries the certainty of ultimate payment. The policyholder who survives the risk of early death is thus saving, not for himself but for others, and it is significant that nearly all forms of saving tend in the final analysis to benefit others than the saver.

Life assurance therefore offers in all its principal forms an opportunity to save for the future *and* secure an interest in the sum to be saved, as protection for the present. At the heart of the system is the life assurance fund in which are pooled all the contributions of a company's policyholders and from which, supplemented by interest and other gains, the benefits are paid in the order that claims arise.

Although life assurance has these two distinct features they are not equally emphasized in every policy. At one extreme there is whole life assurance without profits, in which premiums continue to be paid throughout the policyholder's lifetime. For a given annual sum this provides the maximum immediate cover, which is permanent. At the other extreme is the short-term endowment assurance with profits, which secures for the same annual sum much smaller immediate cover, but in which the bulk of the contributions is paid back, with interest and bonuses, on survival of the term. In between these two main extremes the weight can be shifted towards either present protection or future saving by countless different degrees of emphasis, according to the term and class of policy selected. Thus, if whole life assurance is with profits, immediate cover gives way in part to long-term saving. If premiums are limited in number, a further step is taken in this same direction. At the other end of the scale, by prolonging the period to maturity of endowment assurance, the investment element is reduced and present cover is strengthened.

This range of emphasis gives to modern life assurance its wide latitude of application and makes it possible to devise plans which fulfil a person's requirements at every age. The range is further extended by the new equity-linked contracts which have an important place in the list of policies from which a prospective 'buyer' can now choose.

The object of this book is to treat life assurance on a practical level, to examine its benefits and to suggest ways in which these can be most rewardingly applied. It is, therefore, convenient—even when this means cutting across orthodox divisions—broadly to group the subject-matter according to whether the main object is protective, i.e., to provide cover for dependants, or for investment, i.e., to save for the benefit of the assured. Annuities constitute a third group and these in turn have a special bearing on the problems of retirement and old age. The solution of these problems can involve the whole range of life assurance, which can be deployed to good effect in minimizing both the burden of present taxation and future liability for estate duty.

Where life assurance is concerned, it is not enough to make suggestions; to be of value, they must be supported with examples of costs and benefits and this procedure has been followed in the preparation of this book. At the same time, it must be emphasized that the figures quoted are broadly based on the values offered by a selection of the most competitive companies and are not normally identifiable with the specific terms offered by any one. It is open to argument whether the bonus rates assumed for the purpose of illustration are pitched too high. It is thought that they are not, provided, however, that the net earning capacity of life funds is not unduly handicapped by substantially heavier tax impositions. The effect of the new forms of taxation introduced by the Finance Act, 1965, is considered in Chapter 23.

The earliest contracts of life assurance were temporary assurances to cover the life assured for a period of one year and they were issued by private individuals known as underwriters. The earliest recorded policy was dated 1583 (*see* Chapter 5, p. 48). Life assurance in the various forms in which it is offered today has moved a long way since 1583. There are now over one hundred companies transacting life assurance throughout this country and temporary, or term assurance, ranks as one of the least important classes of policy issued. It has, however, acquired a new significance in convertible term assurance, which includes an option enabling the policyholder to change it later into a permanent contract without evidence of health, and in its decreasing form in connection with loan repayments. The concept of temporary cover with which life assurance was originally identified has been superseded by that of cover lasting for the 'whole of life' (whole life assurance), and by the endowment principle, under which the assured receives the full benefit for which he is covered at the end of an agreed period.

The development of life assurance on a scientific and permanent basis is a natural result of social and economic progress. The more people earn and the greater comforts they enjoy, the more they need to protect their dependants and themselves against the disappearance of those earnings at death or on retirement. But this development would not have taken place on the same scale without the positive encouragement given to life assurance by successive governments. Tax relief was first allowed on life assurance premiums in 1853. Today, when the standard rate of tax is 8*s* 3*d* in the £, the value of this relief is considerable. It means that the person who saves by life assurance, and pays sufficient standard rate of tax to take full advantage of this relief, has for every £ he saves another 3*s* 3½*d* added by the Treasury. Nor is this all. The life fund in which his premiums are pooled and invested to produce the promised benefits and bonuses itself bears tax at a uniform and favourable rate on the interest it earns, currently about 7*s* 6*d* in the £, less expenses. Thus the life assurance policyholder has a good bargain all round compared to other savers.

Since the first edition of this book was published the 1968 Finance Act has been introduced. The Act deserves special mention here because it has had far reaching consequences. But it has not robbed life assurance of its advantages for the normal policyholder. The main impact of the 1968 Finance Act has fallen on the very rich by blocking the operation of life assurance as a means of facile surtax and estate duty avoidance. Many years before 1968 the writing was on the wall and what finally pushed a Socialist government into taking legislative action was probably the intensive and sometimes irresponsible advertising of tax avoidance schemes in the national press.

It may be helpful to summarize here the primary effects of the Act on life assurance.

(*a*) The statutory period for gifts *inter vivos* has been extended from 5 to 7 years.

(*b*) The normal expenditure rules have been redesigned so that to come within the exemption, premiums must be met out of income, leaving the donor's standard of living unchanged; but the test of reasonableness has been dropped. The exemption is specifically excluded where an annuity had been purchased on the deceased's life at any time by way of 'associated operations' as defined by S.59 of Finance Act, 1940.

(*c*) M.W.P.A. and other trust policies, if they are dutiable under S.21(*c*) of Finance Act 1894, are no longer non-aggregable.

(*d*) For premiums under a policy to be eligible for income tax relief the policy must first of all satisfy a number of qualifying conditions. Broadly speaking the policy must be a long-term contract (10 years or more) secured by regular level payments. The policy must of course additionally satisfy the other conditions prescribed in sections 219 and 226 of the Income Tax Act, 1952.

If the policy does not qualify a potential surtax liability is created on the investment proceeds.

(*e*)* Surtax relief is disallowed in respect of interest payments in excess of £100 a year on borrowed moneys regularly applied to pay life assurance premiums.

On 22nd May 1968 Mr Harold Lever, the Financial Secretary to the Treasury, addressed the standing committee A as follows:

'I ought to make it clear that we have no animus against insurance, or any of its branches, or any of its forms. There is no intention to penalize any normal form of insurance.'

This statement is supported by an examination of the effects of the new legislation on the contracts described in the first edition of this book. It will be seen that the normal use of life assurance is virtually unimpeded and only abnormal use is penalized; *in other words the intrinsic merits of life assurance as a means of personal saving and protection for dependants remain as relevant as ever.*

* See Addendum 'Finance Bill, 1969', page 241.

2

Profit Sharing

FROM ITS beginning, the practice of scientific life assurance has given rise to what is technically called 'surplus' and the consequent need for suitable means of distributing it amongst policyholders. Surplus really means more money than is needed to meet the estimated claims. It can arise from a number of sources, such as favourable mortality experience or savings on expenses, but by far the biggest contribution to surplus (other than the additional premium charged for the right to a share of it) is *successful investment*. Surplus is revealed when a company values its life fund, which the Board of Trade requires it to do at least every five years. In practice, most companies make these valuations every three years, and some even annually.

Not all surplus is distributed as profit. Part of it may go to increase reserves which strengthen the life fund against future strains and help to generate profit in the future. But of the distributable profit, normally not less than 90 per cent in the case of proprietary companies (i.e., companies with shareholders who receive dividends out of the surplus) and 100 per cent in the case of mutual companies, belongs to the with-profit policyholders and is paid to them in the form of bonuses.

Since all, or nearly all, classes of policy potentially contribute to surplus, the without-profit policyholders, in effect, help to provide the bonuses distributed to the with-profit policyholders. There are exceptions to this, as in the case where a company keeps a separate participating and non-participating fund, or where all policies of a certain type issued by the company participate. But these exceptions are rare. In the normal way the with-profit policyholder, like an ordinary shareholder in a company which also has preference shares, benefits from 'gearing', i.e., he gets a correspondingly bigger share of the divisible surplus. In practice, this is partially corrected because he is charged a higher premium for the privilege of being in this class. This extra premium is called the 'bonus loading' and might represent an increase of as much as 100 per cent for certain classes of assurance at a young age.

There are only four systems of bonus in use today worth mentioning and of these the first two are by far the most common and will be familiar to most people.

Bonus Systems

Simple Reversionary Bonus

A uniform amount of, say, 70*s* per annum per £100 is added to the sum assured only.

Compound Reversionary Bonus

A uniform amount of, say, 60*s* per annum per £100 is added to the sum assured *and existing bonuses.*

Cash Bonus

The bonus is declared as a cash sum, usually with the option that it can be converted into a reversionary bonus. This method is not popular because a fixed sum of money, when converted into an equivalent addition to the sum assured, produces a smaller reversionary bonus for an old life than for a young life, and policyholders nowadays expect their bonuses to increase as they get older.

Bonuses in Reduction of Premiums

No profits are allotted during the first few years of the policy, but at the end of that period a reduction is made in the premium. Thereafter, smaller reductions are made year by year until no further premiums are payable. Bonuses are then allotted as reversionary additions to the sum assured.

At the present time about 76 per cent of companies use the compound reversionary bonus system and most of the remainder the simple reversionary bonus system.

Discounted Bonus Policies

Some companies are prepared to grant a policy under which future bonuses are anticipated at a suitable rate and applied to reduce the ordinary with-profit premiums. If the bonus declared at valuation is greater than the bonus that has been discounted, the policy is then credited with the difference by addition to the sum assured. If, on the other hand, the declared rate falls short of the discounted rate, either the sum assured is reduced or the premiums are increased to make up the difference.

Simple and Compound Bonuses

It does not need an actuary to see that it is more costly for a company to maintain a compound bonus than a simple bonus of the same magnitude. For this reason, simple bonuses are usually declared at a higher rate. The relative value of these two types of bonus with roughly competitive companies depends to a large extent on the term of the policy. If the policy is for a short term, say a 15-year endowment assurance, a simple bonus paying company is likely to produce the best result. Over longer periods, and this applies particularly to whole life policies taken out at a young age, it is normally wiser to choose a company with a good compound bonus.

The effect of these two principal methods of distributing profits is illustrated below. It is assumed that the basic sum assured in

Position	*Policy 'A'*	*Policy 'B'*
	£	£
At end of 3 years	1,105	1,090
,, ,, ,, 6 years	1,210	1,188
,, ,, ,, 12 years	1,420	1,412
,, ,, ,, 18 years	1,630	1,677
,, ,, ,, 24 years	1,840	1,993
,, ,, ,, 30 years	2,050	2,367
,, ,, ,, 40 years	2,400	3,158

each case is £1,000 and that policy 'A' is credited with a uniform simple bonus of 70*s* per annum, and policy 'B' with a uniform compound bonus of 60*s* per annum declared triennially.

To meet claims occurring between valuations, companies declare an interim rate of bonus which may be slightly more, the same, or slightly less than the last rate. If the interim rate is less than the last declared rate, it is not necessarily a sign that the company lacks confidence in its ability to achieve as good a result at the next valuation. Some companies prefer not to anticipate in full the amount they expect to distribute at the next declaration; which is reasonable, because in the meantime the profit has not been fully earned. But it is fair to assume that, short of an economic catastrophe, the next bonus will be no worse than the interim rate, since no company would make a point of raising expectations in this way if it was not confident it could satisfy them. Events are moving so rapidly today that a company which values its fund as infrequently as every five years may declare more than one interim rate in the interval.

Bonuses that have been allotted can usually be surrendered for their cash value. The cash value of a simple bonus will be less for a young life than for an old one, but will not otherwise be affected by the period for which the policy has been in force. The cash value of a compound bonus will also improve in proportion to the policyholder's age and the length of time the policy has been in force. The cash value of both types of bonus is affected by the original term of the policy. Unless it is unavoidable, it would be foolish to surrender a compound bonus when it is allotted, since the effect of compounding will then be lost. If immediate cash is needed the better course is to borrow from the company against the security of the policy.

Special Bonuses

Since World War II insurance companies have invested an increasing proportion of new money in equities, and the inflationary forces that have operated over this period have substantially increased the earnings of their funds on these and other investments, thus increasing the surplus for distribution as profit. The consequential increase in bonuses, which have reached new record levels at the time this second edition goes to press, have been accompanied in an increasing number of cases by special bonus distributions. The different forms these have taken demonstrate the difficulties which actuaries face in deciding upon the most equitable method of distributing surplus, a problem which has, in fact, teased their minds ever since modern life assurance began. It is too technical to go into here, but behind these special bonus distributions two considerations have been uppermost. One is the desire to reward those policyholders who have contributed most to the exceptional profits realized with more than the normal bonus system allows. The other is the fact that bonus estimates today are frequently taken as being in the nature of promises. A special bonus, if it is clearly labelled as such, is, therefore, less likely to lead to disappointment if it cannot be repeated.

Examples of the various ways these special bonuses have been distributed in very recent years are as follows:

(i) Bonuses on all policies to which normal bonuses had been added.
(ii) Bonuses on all policies that had been in force throughout the whole of the valuation period.
(iii) Additions to policies becoming claims by death or maturity within a fixed period.
(iv) Additions to policies that had been in force for a minimum period of years.

Some of the bonuses described above have been by way of addition to the normal rate of bonus, some have been based only on the sum assured and a few have been dependent in amount on the duration of the policy or on the amount of existing declared bonus.

Future Outlook

In the past the normal reversionary bonus was paid out of the profit from income, rather than from capital gains. Even where special bonuses had been added it is thought that the bulk of these did not arise explicitly from capital appreciation. However, the statements accompanying the most recent declarations (1968) and the form which the special bonuses take clearly suggest that capital appreciation is now being included and if capital values continue to rise in the future it is likely that all companies will bring a portion of this improvement into their distributable surplus. It is reasonable to expect, therefore, that the practice of making special bonus distributions will become firmly established and that as a result the normal bonus will be stabilized to a greater degree. The overall results might be the same, but the distribution of these results would be different.

It can be argued on the other hand that the whole reversionary bonus system is inappropriate to the present structure of insurance companies' investment and that, where life assurance is purely a vehicle for personal saving, it would be better to devise a more personal system of reward. This point of view has led to the introduction of the equity-linked contracts described in Chapter 6. These represent a complete departure from the traditional concept of life assurance and, in some, the element of life assurance exists only as a temporary appendage. In others, the policyholder is protected by a minimum sum assured throughout the duration of the policy.

However, since the first edition of this book was published it is interesting to see how the traditional and equity-linked policy, *which started at different ends of the spectrum* have drawn closer together. Thus it is now becoming common in equity-linked contracts for the sum assured to be guaranteed at maturity, so preserving one of the benefits of a traditional endowment policy. At the same time the trend towards special and terminal bonuses mentioned above has injected into traditional endowment assurance an equity-linked element. The remaining difference is that under the equity-linked policy the gains are not guaranteed as they arise but move freely up and down over the safety net of the sum assured, whereas under the traditional policy once gains are declared they become permanent additions to the sum assured.

3

Life Assurance and Taxation

THE PRINCIPAL tax reliefs at present allowed on premiums to life assurance and annuity contracts may be summarized as follows.

Life Assurance Policies

(Income Tax Act, 1952)

Subject to the qualifying conditions imposed by Finance Act, 1968, the amount at present qualifying for relief of income tax is:

If the total premiums do not exceed £25: *£10 or the amount of premiums, whichever is less.*
If the total premiums exceed £25: *two-fifths of the amount of premiums.*

Policies taken out or changed after 19th March 1968, must be 'qualifying policies' to attract relief. Subject to this relief is given on premiums for life assurances paid by the taxpayer on his own life or that of his wife, or paid by the taxpayer's wife out of her separate income on her own life or that of her husband.

The limits on the amount of premium allowable for tax purposes are determined thus:

(*a*) If the aggregate premiums under all life assurance policies taken out by the taxpayer exceed one-sixth of his total income including that of his wife (after deduction of mortgage interest, ground rent and similar charges), the excess is not eligible for relief.
(*b*) If a premium under a particular policy exceeds 7 per cent of the sum assured (exclusive of any bonuses attaching) relief is only allowed on 7 per cent of the sum assured.

Life assurance funds are taxed at a relatively modest rate and the effect of this, added to income tax relief on premiums, makes a qualifying life assurance policy an attractive investment to anyone paying tax at the current standard rate, and especially so to one who pays surtax.

Finance Act, 1968

For premiums under a policy taken out after 19th March 1968 to be eligible for income tax relief, the policy must first of all satisfy a number of qualifying conditions: i.e. it must be a *qualifying policy*.

If it is not a qualifying policy or if a qualifying policy is prematurely surrendered or altered so that the qualifying conditions are no longer satisfied, a charge to surtax may arise on the investment proceeds.

The Finance Act, 1968, differentiates between policies which were in force on 19th March 1968 and those effected thereafter. The new regulations do not apply to a policy taken out on or before 19th March 1968 unless it is altered after that date so as to 'increase the benefits payable' or to extend the term. Should a policy be so altered then it is treated in the same way as a policy taken out after 19th March 1968 to which the qualifying tests apply. The precise meaning of the phrase 'increase the benefit payable' is not clear in marginal cases but it would include for example the conversion of a whole life assurance to an endowment assurance for the same sum assured.

Qualifying Conditions

Endowment Assurances

(1) The term of the policy must be at least 10 years.

(2) The premiums must be payable annually, or more frequently, over at least 10 years or until the earlier death of the life assured ('premium spread' rule).

(3) The total premiums payable in any 12-month period must not exceed twice the total premiums payable in any other 12-month period ('two times' rule).

(4) The total premiums payable in any 12-month period must not exceed one-eighth of the total premiums payable over the whole term of the policy ('one-eighth' rule).
(5) The guaranteed sum assured payable on death at any time must be at least three-quarters of the total premiums payable to maturity ('75 per cent' rule).

Whole Life Assurances

(1) The premiums must be payable annually, or more frequently, over at least 10 years or until the earlier death of the life assured ('premium spread' rule).
(2) The total premiums payable in any 12-month period must not exceed twice the total premiums payable in any other 12-month period ('two times' rule).
(3) If premiums are limited in number the total premiums payable in any 12-month period must not exceed one-eighth of the total premiums payable ('one-eighth' rule).
(4) If premiums are payable throughout life the total premiums payable in any 12-month period must not exceed one-eighth of the total premiums payable in the first 10 years ('one-eighth' rule).

Temporary Assurances: Term Longer than 10 Years

(1) The premiums must be payable annually, or more frequently, over at least 10 years or for three-quarters of the term if shorter ('premium spread' rule).
(2) The total premiums payable in any 12-month period must not exceed one-eighth of the total premiums payable over the whole term of the policy ('one-eighth' rule).
(3) The total premiums payable in any 12-month period must not exceed one-eighth of the total premiums payable over the whole term of the policy ('one-eighth' rule).

Temporary Assurances: Term 10 Years or Less

The only condition to be satisfied is that the policy must provide that the surrender value cannot exceed the premiums paid: most policies satisfy this rule.

Special Cases

Extra risks

In applying the tests of qualification these are disregarded:

(*a*) Extra premiums payable for medical reasons, occupation or other special hazards.

(*b*) Any debt which is imposed on account of exceptional mortality risk.

Frequency loadings

In applying the '75 per cent' rule the loading for monthly, quarterly and half-yearly premiums is disregarded.

Dating back

For whole life, endowment and temporary assurances, dating back up to and including three months is possible without causing an otherwise qualifying policy to become non-qualifying, because the premium payable at outset in respect of the period of backdating is deemed to have been paid on the effective date.

Dating back more than three months may mean that an otherwise qualifying policy becomes non-qualifying.

Linked policies

If two policies are linked together so that one of them is not allowed to continue unless the other is maintained in force, then for either to be a qualifying policy, each must qualify in its own right and the policies taken together must also qualify.

Application of maturity proceeds

The proceeds of a maturing endowment assurance which was

a qualifying policy (or would have been a qualifying policy had it been effected after 19th March 1968) can be applied to a new policy effected by the original policyholder, and in testing the new policy for qualification:

(*a*) If the new policy is a renewable one and the transfer payment is applied as the first premium or part of the premium on it, then this first premium, or part first premium, is disregarded in applying the 'two times' and 'one-eighth' rules.

(*b*) If the new policy is a single premium one and the single premium consists entirely of the transfer payment, then the 'premium spread', 'two times' and 'one-eighth' rules do not apply.

Conversion of child's deferred assurances

Policies issued on conversion of existing Children's Deferred Assurances and Child's Option Policies will normally be qualifying policies. If the transfer premium, i.e., the cash option under the old policy, is not the only premium payable under the new policy, then the new policy is subject to the normal tests of qualification, except that the transfer premium is disregarded for the purpose of applying the 'two times' rule and the 'one-eighth' rule.

Increasing-premium policies

Policies where there is provision for an automatic increase in the basic premium to more than twice its original amount will not qualify. The existence of an option to increase the premium and convert a whole life to an endowment assurance will not of itself however lead to disqualification of the whole life policy.

Decreasing term assurances

The new rules do not apply to a decreasing term assurance which repays on death the capital outstanding under a repayment mortgage of the life assured's residence, or of any premises occupied by him for the purpose of a business, provided that the sum assured is substantially the same as the amount outstanding under the mortgage.

Income benefits

If a whole life or endowment assurance incorporates Income Benefits it will normally be a qualifying policy.

Pure endowments

Pure endowments are not of course eligible for income tax relief. Since they are not qualifying policies any new pure endowments can now also attract a charge to surtax.

Contingent assurances

Contingent assurances are treated as whole life assurances, and temporary contingent assurances as temporary assurances.

Changed Policies

The following rules apply to both changes and substitutions generally. A policy taken out before 20th March 1968 is not however subject to these rules unless it is being changed (or has, since 19th March 1968, previously been changed) so as to 'increase the benefits payable' or extend the term.

In applying these rules 'old policy' means the original policy as it stands immediately prior to the date of change, and 'new policy' means the policy viewed from the date of change, ignoring past premiums and benefits.

(1) If the old policy does not qualify, the new policy does not qualify (even if, had it not arisen as a result of the change or substitution, it would qualify). Policies issued on conversion of child's deferred assurances are exempted but, apart from this exception, the general effect of this rule is to preclude a non-qualifying policy from being made into a qualifying one. Also it will be observed that if a policy, which has arisen as a result of a M.W.P.A. substitution before 20th March 1968 and which had a large initial premium is changed so as to increase the benefits or extend the term, or is replaced by another, then the new policy will not usually qualify.

(2) If both the new and the old policy satisfy the conditions for qualification, then the new policy qualifies unless:

(*a*) The change or substitution takes place before the old policy has been 10 years in force.

and (*b*) The highest total of premiums payable in any 12-month period under the new policy within 10 years of the start of the old policy is less than one-half of the highest total of premiums paid in any 12-month period under the old policy.

In other words, if disqualification is to be avoided, premiums must normally be paid at the initial level for at least 10 years from outset before they can be reduced by more than one-half.

(3) If the old policy qualifies, but the new policy does not qualify only be reason of its term or because it does not satisfy the 'premium spread', 'two times' or 'one-eighth' rules, the new policy is nevertheless a qualifying policy if:

(*a*) The change or substitution takes place after the old policy has been 10 years in force.

and (*b*) The total premiums paid in any 12-month period under the new policy do not exceed the smallest total of premiums paid in any 12-month period under the old policy.

Thus, if the term of a policy, after it has been 10 years in force, is reduced to less than 10 years from the date of change, it will not be disqualified provided the sum assured is reduced at the same time so that there is no increase in premium.

Notes:

(1) These rules do not apply if the change does not affect the terms of a policy in any significant respect, e.g. a change from annual to monthly premiums or vice versa.

(2) It should be noted that in rules (2) and (3) above the 10-year period runs from the date of the policy, not from the effective date.

(3) It will be seen from the above that generally speaking a policy which has been changed has to satisfy the rules for qualifying policies. In

particular, backdating a change for more than three months may in many cases cause disqualification.

'M.W.P.A. Type' Substitutions

Where the surrender value of a policy is applied as the first premium under a new policy, this first premium may be disregarded in applying the 'two times' and 'one-eighth' rules to the new policy, provided that the policy surrendered has been in force more than 10 years and was (or would have been if it had been effected after 19th March 1968) a qualifying policy, and provided that the new policy is effected by the same person as effected the policy being surrendered. Thus the substitution of a life-of-another policy for an own-life policy cannot secure exemption from the 'two times' and 'one-eighth' rules.

Where the first premium cannot be so disregarded, the new policy can only qualify if the first premium (i.e. the surrender value of the old policy) is small in relation to subsequent premiums.

Surtax Charge on Gains

The policies which become subject to the charge are:

(*a*) All capital redemption policies and purchased life annuities issued after 19th March 1968.
(*b*) Non-qualifying life policies.
(*c*) Qualifying life policies in certain circumstances.

Chargeable Event

The gain arises and surtax becomes chargeable on the happening of a *chargeable event*, which is:

(*a*) *In the case of non-qualifying policies and capital redemption policies*
   (i) Any death which gives rise to benefits under the policy.
   (ii) Maturity of the policy.
   (iii) Surrender of the policy at any time.

(iv) The assignment of the policy for money or money's worth.

(*b*) *In the case of qualifying policies*

(i) Any of the above events but only if the policy has previously been made paid-up within 10 years of outset or three-quarters of the term if less.

(ii) Surrender of the policy within that time.

(iii) The assignment of the policy for money or money's worth within that time.

(*c*) *In the case of purchased life annuities*

(i) Surrender of the annuity including the taking of the cash option at vesting of a deferred annuity.

(ii) The assignment of the annuity for money or money's worth.

Notes:

(1) Surrender of bonus does not itself give rise to a surtax charge.

(2) The period of 10 years runs from the date of the policy and not the effective date. It appears therefore that if a qualifying policy had been dated back the policyholder may have to pay more than 10 years' premiums before making his policy fully-paid if he is to avoid the possibility of a surtax charge.

(3) An assignment effected by way of security for a debt or a reassignment on repayment thereof, or an assignment between spouses living together, is disregarded.

(4) A policy which has been changed in such a way as to increase the premiums payable, and which is a qualifying policy, will be treated for the purpose of determining whether a chargeable event has occurred as if it were a qualifying policy effected at the date of change. In particular, therefore, surrender within 10 years of the date of change of a policy converted from whole life to endowment assurance may be a chargeable event.

Calculation of Gain

The amount of the gain chargeable to surtax in respect of life policies is the amount by which the total premiums paid (including any extra premiums paid for medical reasons, etc.) is exceeded by:

In the case of a death

The surrender value immediately before death (plus the cash value of any bonuses previously surrendered):

In the case of a maturity, surrender or assignment

The total sums paid (including the cash value of any bonuses previously surrendered), a partial surrender giving rise to the appropriate proportionate gain.

If the policy has been issued in substitution for another, the references to bonuses and premiums include those on the substituted policy.

Corresponding provisions apply to annuities and capital redemption policies.

Calculation of Surtax

The whole gain, computed as above, will be deemed for the purposes of surtax to be income of the policyholder in the fiscal year in which the chargeable event took place. The gain will be deemed to form part of the policyholder's income irrespective of whether the policy is vested in him as beneficial owner or is held on trusts (M.W.P.A., etc.) created by him, but in the latter case he can recover the surtax from the trustees out of the benefits received by them on the happening of the event.

The rate of surtax is determined by the method of 'top-slicing', i.e. by dividing the gain by the number of complete years for which the policy has run, and finding the rate of surtax which would be payable thereon as if it constituted the highest part of the policyholder's total income for the year in which the chargeable event arose. This rate of surtax is then applied to the whole of the chargeable gain.

It will be appreciated that only if the policyholder is a surtax payer, or becomes a surtax payer through the addition of the appropriate slice of gain to his income, will he in fact be liable to surtax on any gain. Moreover, a policy issued on or before 19th March 1968 cannot give rise to a surtax charge unless it is changed after that date so as to increase the benefits or extend the term.

Interest on Loans to pay Premiums

New provisions (*see* Addendum 'Finance Bill, 1969', page 241) apply to loans made after 19th March 1968, whether on security of a life policy or otherwise. Where such a loan is used directly or indirectly for the payment of premiums on a life policy, the interest on the loan is *not* a deduction for surtax purposes unless:

(*a*) Interest is payable at a rate not exceeding 10 per cent per annum.

and (*b*) Neither the first premium under the policy, nor the total premiums subsequently payable in any 12-month period, exceeds one-eighth of the sum assured.

and (*c*) It is shown to the satisfaction of the Inland Revenue that it is exceptional for the policyholder to apply borrowed money to the payment of premiums, and that no such money has been applied by him in any of the three previous fiscal years.

Subject to (*a*) above being satisfied, there is an exemption for interest of not more than £100 gross per annum, provided the policy is either subject to level premiums payable annually or more frequently, or is a qualifying policy.

Capital Gains Tax

Under the Finance Act, 1965, the proceeds of *normal* life policies are exempt from capital gains tax. An exception to a normal life policy is a capital redemption policy, but this is a relatively unimportant section of business. The tax is, however, payable on the proceeds of normal life policies in the hands of a purchaser who is not the original beneficial owner, and considerable care may be needed to ensure that certain legitimate transactions are not accidentally caught by this provision.

Purchased Life Annuities
(Finance Act, 1956)

Section 27 of the Finance Act, 1956, provides that where an annuity is purchased by an annuitant out of his own capital resources, a part of the annuity will be regarded as representing a return of the purchase price as distinct from interest on it and will be exempt from tax. The capital element, as this tax-free portion is called, varies according to age and sex. Some examples are given in Chapter 7. This relief is not allowed on any annuity purchased in pursuance of any direction in a will or under a court order, or on a deferred annuity where any relief of income tax has been allowed on the premium.

Deferred Annuities for the Self-employed and Others

(Finance Act, 1956)

Sections 22 and 23 of the Finance Act, 1956, extend a measure of superannuation justice to self-employed persons, most controlling directors and employees not in pensionable employment. Until the passing of this Act, a person who was not eligible to join a superannuation fund approved under S.379 Income Tax Act, 1952, could obtain only the relief of tax allowed for life assurance premiums, i.e., income tax (not surtax) relief on two-fifths of premiums paid towards old age provision. A member of a superannuation fund approved under S.379 could, on the other hand, obtain tax relief in effect on seven-ninths of his contributions as an employee. Under this legislation, premiums to approved contracts rank as a charge against income for both income tax and surtax, whilst the emerging pension, which cannot be commuted, is taxed as earned income. A further point is that the investment income of the insurance company derived from these premiums is free of tax. Consequently, better than average rates are quoted.

Approved Contracts

In order to obtain Inland Revenue approval, the contract must fulfil certain conditions. It must have as its main object the provision for the person concerned of a life annuity to commence sometime between the ages of 60 and 70. The annuity cannot be commuted for a lump sum, nor can a lump sum be paid on death before the pension becomes payable, except insofar as this represents a return of the premiums paid and accumulated at a moderate rate of interest. No surrender or assignment is permitted. Instead of a return of premiums on death, an annuity can be provided for the widow (or widower) so long as this does not exceed the amount of the annuity that would otherwise be paid to the contributor.

The Inland Revenue, however, have certain discretionary powers to approve contracts which make provision for (i) an annuity to a dependant other than a widow or widower; (ii) an annuity commencing before the age of 60 in the event of incapacity to carry on working or where retirement before the age of 60 is common in the occupation, and (iii) an annuity guaranteed payable for up to ten years irrespective of whether the annuitant survives the guaranteed term.

Relevant Earnings

The 'relevant earnings' referred to in the Act, on which relief is allowed, are income arising in respect of remuneration for an office or employment of profit other than one which is already pensionable. They include income chargeable under Schedules B or D, derived from the practice of a trade, profession or vocation.

Limits Allowed

(*a*) If the contributor was born in 1916 or later, relief is given on contributions not exceeding one-tenth of his net relevant earnings and £750.

(*b*) To allow for the fact that older persons are at a disadvantage on this basis compared to younger persons who have an opportunity to contribute for a longer period from the time of the Act, the earnings and contribution limits on which relief can be obtained are extended for those born before 1916 on the following scale:

Year of birth	*Percentage of Net relevant earnings (per cent)*	*Overriding maximum (£)*
1914 or 1915	11	825
1912 or 1913	12	900
1910 or 1911	13	975
1908 or 1909	14	1,050
1907 or earlier	15	1,125

The limits in (*a*) above still apply, however, to a person born in 1915 or earlier in any year of assessment in which he receives a pension or retains pension rights from previous employment.

'Net relevant earnings' are relevant earnings less any charges payable out of income or capital or other allowances which reduce income for tax purposes.

An important point about these statutory limits is that premiums disallowed in any year because of insufficiency of earnings may be carried forward to the next year, if earnings in that year are sufficient to support them.

The relative advantages of securing a retirement pension under these provisions and through an endowment policy subject to normal life assurance tax reliefs are considered in Chapter 16. The special contracts designed to meet the requirements of the Act are described in Chapter 7 and illustrated in Chapter 18.

4

Life Assurance and Estate Duty

THE FINANCE ACT, 1894, charges to estate duty the principal value of all property passing, or deemed to pass, at death. None of the heads under which duty is charged refer exclusively to life policies but, in practice, a life assurance or annuity policy could be dutiable in any one of the following three ways under the provisions of the Act.

(*1*) *Because it forms part of the life assured's estate*

If the policy belonged to the life assured at the time of his death, then it is property passing at his death and is dutiable in the same way as the rest of his property under S.1 of the Act. The property in question is the policy itself, and the principal value of that property is the sum assured, plus any bonuses. If the policy does not belong to the life assured at the time of death, then the property does not pass and no duty is chargeable under this section, although a claim for duty may arise for one of the other reasons given below.

(*2*) *Because it was the subject of a gift within seven years of death*

If the policy belonged to the deceased and he gave it away or retained an interest in it within seven years of his death, then it is dutiable under S.2(1)(*c*) like any other gift. As in (1) above the policy moneys will be aggregable with the rest of the donor's estate. S.64 of the Finance Act, 1960 as amended by Finance Act, 1968, provides that if a gift is survived by more than four years the value of the gift on which duty is assessed is reduced by 15 per cent after four years, 30 per cent after five years, and 60 per cent after six years. S.34 of the Finance Act, 1959, provides that *the value* of the policy on which duty is assessed will be calculated by taking the proportion of the total premiums paid before the gift to the total of all premiums paid and applying this to the benefits receivable at maturity.

The following example illustrates how this works. 'A' takes out a policy on his own life for £1,000 and pays nine premiums, then gives it to 'B' who pays six premiums before 'A' dies, and the policy matures for payment to 'B'. The total premiums paid before the gift represent three-fifths of the total of all premiums paid. Accordingly, the property deemed to pass is valued at three-fifths of the total proceeds of the policy, which is £600. Since the gift has been survived by more than six years, S.64 of the Finance Act, 1960, as amended by Finance Act, 1968, operates to reduce the value by 60 per cent. The result is that duty is charged on £240. Since the policy belonged to 'A' at one time, the sum in question would be aggregable with the rest of 'A's' estate.

Under S.33 of the Finance Act, 1949, gifts not exceeding £500 to any one donee are exempt from duty, but the exemption does not apply in the above example because the value of the policy *at the date it was given* was £600.

(3) *Because it was purchased or provided by the deceased*

Section (2)(1)(*d*) charges duty on an 'annuity or other interest purchased or provided by the deceased ... to the extent of the beneficial interest accruing or arising by survivorship or otherwise on the death of the deceased'. Under S.1 of the Act, it is the policy which attracts duty and the test is whether the policy belonged to the deceased at the date of death. Under this section, the subject of duty is in effect a change of title in the policy, which gives rise to the beneficial interest. A common case of this used to be where a husband settled a policy on his wife if she should survive him, and, if not, in trust for the children. But under English law as a result of the Kilpatrick decision it is now held that the wife had an interest in possession.

S.34, Finance Act, 1959

A life policy may also be dutiable under S.34 of the Finance Act, 1959. This covers the case of a policy which the deceased effected on his own life and kept up (by continuing to pay premiums) for the benefit of another. Before this Act, duty would have been charged under (2) above (except that the whole proceeds of the policy would have been dutiable) but the provisions of S.2(1)(*c*) were found to operate harshly in certain cases of this kind and the object of the 1959 legislation was to treat the payment of premiums, where appropriate, like any other gifts for the purposes of estate duty. But it does not in any way exempt policies which are liable for duty under the three sections discussed above.

The *kept up* policy may be one which the deceased originally effected in his own name and subsequently assigned to the donee, or one which he originally effected in trust for the benefit of the donee; for example, a policy effected under the provisions of the Married Women's Property Act for the absolute benefit of his wife. In either event, the section applies to the premiums paid by the deceased within seven years of his death. In the former case, the gift of the policy will be dutiable under (2) above and this section will operate on the premiums paid subsequent to the gift; in the latter case, duty will be wholly charged under this section. For the purposes of the section each premium payment is treated as a gift of 'rights under the policy', and these rights are valued at the date of death in the way explained in (2) above, so that each payment of a premium causes a corresponding part of the policy to become liable for duty.

Sections 35 to 38 Finance Act, 1968

Rules for Gifts

Under the previous legislation the statutory period for gifts *inter vivos* was five years, with tapering off in the third, fourth and fifth year. If the amount dutiable had, by 19th March 1968, already been reduced by the operation of the old legislation, the new legislation will not increase it again. Consider for example a gift made on 25th December 1964. If the donor had died on 19th March 1968 the gift would have been taken at 70 per cent of its value for estate duty purposes. It will, therefore, remain at that level for two years longer than before, i.e. until 24th December

1970, and then reduce to 40 per cent in the seventh year; it will not increase to 100 per cent the rate applicable in the fourth year under the rules for new gifts. In particular, this applies to gifts of rights made by the payment of premiums under trust policies effected before 20th March 1966.

Normal Expenditure

The Finance Act, 1910, exempted from duty gifts 'which are proved to the satisfaction of the Commissioners to have been part of the normal expenditure of the deceased, and to have been reasonable, having regard to the amount of his income, or to the circumstances'. Instead of this, the 1968 Act provides that in respect of gifts made after 19th March 1968, exemption will apply 'if it is shown to the satisfaction of the Board (i.e. the Commissioners of Inland Revenue) or, on an appeal under Section 10 of the Finance Act 1894, of the Court entertaining the appeal, that the gift was part of the normal expenditure of the deceased, that the deceased made the gift out of his income and that, after allowing for all gifts forming part of his normal expenditure, the deceased was left with sufficient income to maintain his usual standard of living'.

In the case of trust policies dutiable under Section 2(1)(*c*) of the Finance Act, 1894, it appears that gifts for the purpose of this test are intended to be taken as the premiums paid. It will be noted that premiums paid from capital after 19th March 1968, which used to be able to qualify, will no longer do so.

'Combined Scheme' Arrangements

The Act provides that payment of a premium after 19th March 1968 on a policy on the life of the deceased (or any gift of money or money's worth applied directly or indirectly in payment of such a premium) shall not be regarded as normal expenditure of the deceased if any annuity on the life of the deceased is purchased at the same time as the policy was effected, or at any other time, unless it can be shown that the effecting of the policy and the annuity were not 'associated operations' (as defined in Section 59 of the Finance Act, 1940). This provision prevents the premiums paid after 19th March 1968, on a policy which forms part of the usual 'combined scheme', from securing the benefit of exemption under the 'normal expenditure' rule. It is believed that the combination of the above legislation with Section 44 of the Finance Act, 1940, will also prevent a 'combined scheme' from being operated with the policy on 'life-of-another' basis.

Interpretation of Wording

'Income' is not defined in the Act. It has been stated that, in this context, income would include the capital element of a purchased life annuity and that it means broadly income on accountancy principles, after tax, but this statement is not the equivalent of a legal definition.

The term 'normal' will also be for the Courts to interpret, but in the case of straightforward life assurances the Inland Revenue have indicated their willingness to recognize that, by entering into a contract which envisages regular payments, the policyholder is from the outset taking on the premiums as part of his normal expenditure.

It is reasonable to expect that most normal policies taken out with the intention of providing for the life assured's dependants will be able to claim exemption from duty under the 'normal expenditure' rule.

It is significant that the old exemption applicable to gifts made before 20th March 1968 was discretionary. The new exemption may be claimed by anyone who can satisfy the Court that the case comes within the terms of Section 37 of the Act.

£500 Exemption

This has not been changed by the Act except that the total gifts to any one donee must now not exceed £500 during seven instead of five years before death.

In determining whether exemption applies in the case of a gifted policy, the value of the gift relevant to each premium is calculated. For a given premium the value of the gift is that proportion of the market value of the policy (after payment of the premium) which the amount of that premium bears to all premiums which have by then been paid.

Non-aggregation

Any property (including gifted policies or interests therein), which under Section 2(1)(*c*) of the Finance Act, 1894, passes on death, will now for the purposes of aggregation be considered to be property in which the deceased had an interest, and it will therefore be aggregated with the rest of his property for the purpose of determining the rate of estate duty. An annuity becoming payable on the death of the deceased, i.e. a reversionary annuity, will be treated for this purpose as a policy of assurance.

Policies effected before 20th March 1968

Gifted policies effected before 20th March 1968 are excluded from the new rules and may thus still obtain the benefit of non-aggregation, if:

(*a*) The policy is 'related to the death'.

and (*b*) The total amount payable under all policies 'related to death' effected before 20th March 1968 does not exceed £25,000. This does not include policies which had matured or had been surrendered before 20th March 1968.

A policy is 'related to the death': if it is a policy on the life of the deceased, if property comprised in a gift of, or of rights under, the policy passes on the death, and if that property would under the old legislation have been property in which the deceased never had an interest. All gifted policies on the deceased's life are thus included except those in which he had an interest.

If the total benefits payable exceed £25,000, a proportion, being the proportion which £25,000 bears to the total amount of the benefits, will be treated specially and will be subject to the rules for non-aggregation which were in force before the passing of the Finance Act, 1968. The remainder will be aggregable with the rest of the deceased's estate. The rate of duty payable on the £25,000 slice may, however, be higher than if the £25,000 were the totality of the separate estate, because the rate will be related to the total of the dutiable benefits.

Changes to policies effected before 20th March 1968

If the terms of a policy are changed after 19th March 1968 in such a way that the value of the policy is greater than it would have been if no change had been made, the relief from the new rules for aggregation described above will be restricted. In particular, therefore, it should be observed that if a gifted policy is converted from without-profit to with-profit after 19th March 1968, a proportion (in some cases the whole) of any bonuses payable on a death claim may be aggregated even though the total amount payable under all policies 'related to the death' does not exceed £25,000. (Policies which are exempt from duty under normal expenditure, £500 exemption or marriage consideration are not included for this purpose.)

Life of Another

A policy effected by a wife on her husband's life (or vice versa) does not appear to be affected by the provisions of the Act regarding estate duty provided that it is neither a gifted policy nor forms part of a 'combined scheme', i.e. is associated with an annuity on the husband's life. There will be no duty payable on the policy proceeds, but if the husband has to give his wife the money to pay the premiums these payments will be dutiable as gifts of cash in accordance with the usual rules relating to such gifts: they may, of course, secure exemption under the 'normal expenditure' rule or otherwise.

Trust Policies

There are still considerable advantages to be gained from the writing of policies under the M.W.P.A. and similar trusts because, although these policies will no longer have the benefit of non-aggregation, this will only be relevant if they are dutiable. In many cases, a policy will be exempted from duty altogether because the premiums are regarded as forming part of the 'normal expenditure' of the deceased. Even if the policy is dutiable, duty may be payable on only a part of the proceeds.

Contingent Interests: Kilpatrick Decision

It often happens that a Married Women's Property Act policy is made payable to the wife if she survives the assured and failing that to the children absolutely. It was long held in this case that there was a shift in the beneficial interest at the time of death from a contingent interest to a vested interest, with the result that duty was chargeable under S.2(1)(*d*) (see 3 above). In effect this meant that duty was chargeable on the whole value of the policy with no relief in respect of the part corresponding to premiums survived by the statutory period (previously five and now seven years). This was challenged in the Kilpatrick case (1966). The Kilpatrick case was concerned with a number of policies where the trust took a particular and perhaps not very usual form; but the underlying principles apply to many other policies under which duty would previously have been claimed under S.2(1)(*d*). The Kilpatrick ruling established that in the example cited the wife has an interest vested in possession from the commencement of the assurance so that on the husband's death the wife being still alive, duty is chargeable under S.2(1)(*c*), which is usually more favourable. In other words the position is the same, if the husband predeceases his wife, as if the policy had been effected for the absolute benefit of the wife. If however the wife predeceased her husband there would be this difference: the trustees of the policy would be accountable for the duty concurrently with the beneficiary, (whereas if the policy was for the absolute benefit of the wife then on her death her personal representatives would be accountable). In both cases duty is chargeable on the market value of the policy at the date of death under S.1 of Finance Act, 1894.

It would appear that the same principles apply if on the death of the wife in the lifetime of the husband the policy reverted to the husband instead of going over to the children or some other third party.

It is understood, however, that the Kilpatrick decision only applies under English law, and not to policies governed by Scots law. In consequence, policies of the type 'for A when failing for B' continue to be dutiable under S.2(1)(*d*) of Finance

Act, 1894, where 'A' and 'B' are both alive at the assured's death.

Married Women's Property Act, 1882

The Married Women's Property Act, 1882, applies to England, Wales and Northern Ireland but not to Scotland, which has its own statute, the Married Women's Policies of Assurance Act, 1880. The provisions of the Acts are much the same and what is said below applies to both, with the very important exception that the facilities afforded by the Scottish Act are still only available to men.

A policy may be effected under S.2 of the Act by a man assuring his own life for the benefit of his wife and/or children, or by a woman assuring her life for the benefit of her husband and/or children. The Adoption Act, 1958, extends the possible beneficiaries to legally adopted children, but this Act does not apply in Northern Ireland. The Act does not extend to step-children, grandchildren or other relatives. A policy effected under the provisions of the Married Women's Property Act offers the following advantages:

(i) It creates an immediate trust in favour of the beneficiaries, thus avoiding the trouble and expense of executing a separate deed.

(ii) Because the trust is immediate, each premium counts as a gift of rights in the policy *ab initio*, with possible exemption from duty of all or part of the policy proceeds.

(iii) It enables the insurance company to make immediate payment of the policy moneys to the appointed trustees on proof of death without waiting for a Grant of Probate or Letters of Administration.

(iv) It protects the beneficiaries against claims that might be made by creditors of the policyholder, so long as it cannot be proved that the policy was effected with intent to defraud them.

The following are some examples of the various forms in which a policy may be written under the Married Women's Property Act and some of the estate duty consequences.

By Husband

(*a*) *For the absolute benefit of his wife*

The wife is named in the policy and she takes an immediate vested interest in the policy. As a result of the husband's death the policy moneys are dutiable under S.34 Finance Act, 1959, each premium being treated as a gift of rights in the policy. The gift exemptions will apply.

(*b*) *For the benefit of his wife if she survives him; otherwise for named children absolutely*

(i) *Death of husband while wife is alive*

English Law:

As a result of the Kilpatrick decision the wife has a vested interest in possession and duty is chargeable under S.34 of Finance Act, 1959, as in (*a*) above. The gift exemptions will apply. Prior to the Kilpatrick decision the policy moneys would have been dutiable under S.2(1)(*d*) of Finance Act, 1894, on the grounds that the wife's interest was contingent and vested on the husband's death.

Scots Law:

Duty is chargeable under S.2(1)(*d*) on the whole of the policy moneys. No gift exemptions apply.

(ii) *Death of wife while husband is alive*

English Law:

Duty is payable on the market value of the policy under S.1 Finance Act, 1894. Prior to the Kilpatrick decision, no duty would have been payable as the wife's interest was regarded as a contingent one which failed on her predeceasing her husband.

Scots Law:

No claim for duty as wife's interest is treated as having failed.

(*c*) *For the benefit of his wife if she survives him; otherwise for the husband*

(i) *Death of husband while wife is alive*

English Law:

Duty claimed under S.34 Finance Act, 1959. Gift exemptions will apply.

Scots Law:

Duty under S.2 (1)(*d*).

(ii) *Death of wife in lifetime of husband*

English Law:

Duty on market value of policy under S.1 Finance Act, 1894.

Scots Law:

No claim for duty.

(*d*) *For such of* (*a*), (*b*), (*c*) *and* (*d*) *(being wife and children) as the husband shall by deed or will appoint and, failing such appointment, for the benefit of* (*a*) *absolutely*

(i) *Death of husband without having made an appointment*

English Law:

(*a*) has a vested interest in possession subject to defeasance, which becomes indefeasible on the husband's death but the change in (*a*)'s interest does not give rise to a claim under S.2(1)(*d*). Duty is therefore payable under S.34 Finance Act, 1959.

Scots Law:

Duty payable under S.34 Finance Act, 1959.

(ii) *Death of husband after making a revocable appointment to (b)*

English Law:

(*b*) has a vested interest in possession subject to defeasance should the appointment in his favour be revoked. Duty payable under S.34 Finance Act, 1959.

Scots Law:

If the appointment was by deed the duty is claimed under S.34 Finance Act, 1959; if the appointment was by will, duty claimed under S.2(1)(*d*).

By Wife

A policy may be written by a married woman in her own name and on her own life for the benefit of husband and children in all the ways described above. She may also effect a policy on the life of her husband. In this case no trust is created but the policy is subject to the Married Women's Property Act to the extent that the Act empowers a married woman to hold property which is protected from her husband's creditors and to contract in her own right. A policy written in this form is therefore the sole and absolute property of the wife.

Trustees

The Act contemplates the appointment of trustees. Trustees can be appointed by the policy or by a memorandum under hand. Most insurance companies supply their own forms of request and appointment for this purpose. The insured may appoint whom he wishes as trustees so long as the persons appointed are of full age and consent to the appointment. A popular practice is for the insured to appoint himself and his wife as trustees. On the death of the husband the policy moneys can then be paid to his wife as surviving trustee, on production of the policy and a death certificate. By including himself as trustee, the husband retains some measure of control over the policy during his lifetime.

If trustees are not appointed, the Act provides that payment will be made to the assured's legal personal representatives, as trustees

Current Rates of Estate Duty*

Principal value of estate			*Amount of duty*	
Exceeding (£)	*Not exceeding* (£)	*Rate of duty* (£)	*From* (£)	*To* (£)
—	5,000	nil	—	—
5,000	6,000	1	1	60
6,000	7,000	2	61	140
7,000	8,000	3	141	240
8,000	10,000	4	241	400
10,000	12,500	6	401	750
12,500	15,000	8	751	1,200
15,000	17,500	10	1,201	1,750
17,500	20,000	12	1,751	2,400
20,000	25,000	15	2,401	3,750
25,000	30,000	18	3,751	5,400
30,000	35,000	21	5,401	7,350
35,000	40,000	24	7,351	9,600
40,000	45,000	28	9,601	12,600
45,000	50,000	31	12,601	15,500
50,000	60,000	35	15,501	21,000
60,000	75,000	40	21,001	30,000
75,000	100,000	45	30,001	45,000
100,000	150,000	50	45,001	75,000
150,000	200,000	55	75,001	110,000
200,000	300,000	60	110,001	180,000
300,000	500,000	65	180,001	325,000
500,000	750,000	70	325,001	525,000
750,000	1,000,000	75	525,001	750,000
1,000,000		80	750,001	

Notes: (1) These rates are reduced by 45 per cent in the case of agricultural property and certain business assets, such as factory premises and machinery.

(2) When the value of the estate does not greatly exceed the figure in the first column, 'marginal relief' is allowed. For example, if the value of the estate is £62,000 the duty is 35 per cent of £60,000 (= £21,000) plus the whole of the excess over £60,000, i.e., £2,000, making a total of £23,000 instead of £24,800 (40 per cent of £64,000).

* See Addendum 'Finance Bill, 1969' page 241.

with the duty to carry out the terms of the trust set out in the policy.

The proposal form is signed by the person who is effecting the policy, *not* by the trustees and *not* by the beneficiary.

The trustees are accountable for any estate duty payable in respect of the policy and are entitled to deduct such duty before making payment to the beneficiaries.

Alteration of Policy

The terms of the trust under a policy written under the Act cannot be altered after the policy has been effected, nor can the policy be surrendered or borrowed against without the consent of the beneficiary, unless the insured had given the trustees these specific powers at outset.

The various powers which should be given to trustees, particularly where minor beneficiaries are involved, include the following:

(1) To convert the policy at any time to paid-up assurance for a reduced amount or to surrender the policy.

(2) To borrow on the security of the policy in order to pay any overdue or future premiums and expenses incurred in such borrowing.

(3) To exercise any of the options contained in the policy; to convert the policy into any other forms of assurance on the life of the contributor; to increase or decrease the amount of the annual premium payable thereunder; to alter the period during which the premium is payable, and to do any of these things notwithstanding that the sum assured may thereby be reduced, subject always to the insurance company's practice in the normal course of business at that time.

(4) To invest the proceeds of the policy in any investments (whether authorized for the investment of trust moneys or not) upon which they may decide as if they were the beneficial owners thereof.

In exercising these options, of course, care must be taken that a charge for surtax does not arise under Finance Act, 1968.

Application of the 1959 and 1960 Finance Acts on Life Policies effected after 19th March 1968

In the case of policies becoming 'claims' whilst level annual premiums are being paid, the duty liability is as follows:

Number of equal annual premiums paid	*Dutiable and aggregable proportion of policy moneys (per cent)*
1	100
2	100
3	100
4	100
5	97
6	$92\frac{1}{2}$
7	85
8	$74\frac{3}{8}$
9	$66\frac{1}{9}$
10	$59\frac{1}{2}$
20	$29\frac{3}{4}$
	and so on

The general formula applicable, once seven years' premiums have been paid, for deriving the proportion of the proceeds which is dutiable and aggregable, is 5·95 divided by the number of years' premiums which have been paid.

Part Two

POLICIES AND THEIR USES

5

Primarily for Protection

Whole Life Assurance

In its original form, whole life assurance provides that in return for a premium payable throughout life the sum assured shall be payable at death, whenever that may occur. It is the purest form of permanent life assurance contract and, if the policy is taken out without profits, offers the cheapest method of establishing *permanent* protection for dependants. If the policy is with profits, the amount payable on death is the sum assured plus any bonuses which have been added.

Permanent cover may not seem so important to a young man who is more concerned with his immediate responsibilities than future needs, but it counts for a lot later on in life when the chances of passing a medical examination are less favourable. It is necessary to emphasize this because of the undoubted bias in this country, though not in North America, towards endowment assurance, which is frequently taken out when whole life assurance would serve the purpose better.

It is possible that someone who takes out whole life assurance at a young age to safeguard the future may find, later on, that the cover is no longer needed. His circumstances may have changed or may not have developed as was originally expected. This is not an argument against a young person entering into a permanent contract of this nature, because reasonable surrender values are usually allowed in whole life assurance after only a few years' premiums have been paid. As an alternative to surrendering the policy, premiums can be discontinued and the policy left in force for a reduced sum assured. If the policy participates in profits and has been maintained for a long time, it may be found that the bonus additions exceed the difference between the original sum assured and the paid-up sum assured, so that the original benefit of the policy has been fully preserved. Moreover, many policies provide that the paid-up sum assured continues to participate in profits. A number of companies are now willing to guarantee minimum surrender values and some will endorse on the policy the actual surrender value attaching from time to time.

Thus, whilst whole life assurance is in the nature of a permanent contract, the policyholder, but not the company, is free to cancel it at his discretion and if he exercises this discretion he does not automatically forfeit all rights or necessarily waste his past contributions. But, having made this point, it should be added that whole life assurance cannot be given up at an early stage without some financial loss.

There are a number of variations on the traditional form of this policy and these are considered below.

Whole Life Assurance With Limited Premiums

Premiums are limited to a fixed number or cease on attainment of a specified age, often 65. This modification increases the annual cost, though not necessarily the total cost, depending on the date of death. For example, for a man aged 30 next birthday the annual cost of a non-profit whole life assurance for £3,000 with premiums payable throughout life is about £37, whereas if premiums cease at the age of 65 the corresponding cost is about £41. Whole life assurance with limited premiums appeals to people who like to feel that they will be free of certain household expenses, including life assurance premiums, when they retire. The surrender values allowed for this type of contract are usually liberal, and it is common practice for companies to grant paid-up policies for amounts bearing the same proportion to the original sum assured as the number of years' premiums paid bears to the maximum number originally payable. It is often more sensible, however, to concentrate at the outset on providing maximum cover for the premium that can be afforded, and to convert the policy to limited premiums at a later date. If the policy is with profits, its conversion to a paid-up assurance at the age of 65 will involve only a small reduction in the sum assured. The bonuses that have accrued will be unaffected and, after a run of 35 years, these could be very substantial indeed.

Optional Whole Life Assurance

For the first period of the assurance the ordinary whole of life rate of premium is charged and at the end of the period specified the policyholder has an option to convert the policy to an endowment assurance for any one of various terms of years. In practice, it is always possible for a person to convert his whole of life into endowment assurance, provided he is prepared to take a risk on the exact terms of conversion. This is because the company is not adding to its risk but diminishing it.

The inclusion of the option is therefore of little or no value except as an aid to the salesman.

Another option which is frequently made available does expose the insurance company to additional risk. The object of this is to enable a young policyholder to add more cover as he needs it, without having to submit to further medical examination. For instance, the option may provide that additional assurances can be taken out at the end of the third, fourth and fifth years of the original policy, usually without evidence of health apart from a brief statement. The additional cover allowed on these terms is limited to a proportion, which might be 50 per cent, of the original sum assured.

Equity-linked Whole Life Assurance and Estate Duty Funding

Life assurance is almost the only practicable way in which a sum of money can be provided at death without the forced realization of securities. It follows, therefore, that whole life assurance, in addition to its broader purposes, affords a very satisfactory method of providing for death duties.

Clause 37 of Finance Act, 1968, allows exemption from estate duty of gifts which were part of the deceased's normal expenditure. By taking advantantage of this it is possible to set up a whole life policy written in trust for named beneficiaries, the whole of the proceeds of which will be available free of charge to pay the duty on the rest of the estate. The policy should be taken out for an initial sum assured sufficient to cover the estimated duty on current rates on the present value of the estate. But, of course, in a period of inflation the estate is likely to increase considerably in value as the years go by, assuming that it consists largely of equity shares or assets such as property with equity features. It is logical in these circumstances to choose a policy the value of which is likely to follow the same trends. This would be an equity-linked whole life policy in preference to a traditional with-profits policy, since the value of the latter is not directly determined by the market price of equities from time to time.

Recently some very good contracts have been introduced, under which the sum assured is linked to the value of the units in a fund largely invested in ordinary shares, subject to a guaranteed minimum which is nearer the basic sum assured obtainable under a non-profit than the normal with-profit policy. One of these is illustrated in Plan XXXIII.

An unfamiliar use of whole life assurance is in connection with house purchase—*see* Chapter 12.

Term Assurance

Term assurance, or temporary assurance as it is sometimes called, is, in fact, life assurance in its oldest form (*see* p. 5). In his *History of British Insurance*, Mr Harold E. Raynes cites as the earliest known life assurance policy one which was dated 18 June 1583, and issued for twelve months on the life of William Gibbons for £382 6*s* 8*d* at a rate of £8 per cent. Later, the practice grew up of assuring the lives of well-known people for short periods at premium rates which varied according to their reputed health and the chances of death by misadventure. Term assurance lends itself to this type of speculation, but it has been curbed since the Life Assurance Act, 1774, commonly called the 'Gambling Act', made it illegal to insure someone's life unless the person taking out the policy had a pecuniary interest in the assured's survival.

Term assurance, then, provides for payment of the sum assured only if death occurs within a specified period. Consequently, it contains very little or no element of investment. It may be issued for terms ranging from a few months to several years, and is invariably without profits. This, and the fact that the policy normally carries no surrender value, makes it an unattractive proposition for any long-term commitment, but in its *decreasing* form, which is discussed below, it is useful to cover repayment of a loan, as, for example, in the case of a mortgage through a building society. The chief purpose of term assurance, therefore, is to cover a special risk of relatively short duration, as in the case of a trip abroad, a short-term loan, or some other situation where for a time the risk of death, or the financial consequences of it, are magnified.

It is worth noting that, because of the initial expenses involved in setting up the policy, a term assurance for less than one year cannot be granted at a *pro rata* premium. The premium charged for, say, six months' cover would normally be about three-quarters of that for a full year. If a medical examination is required, the cost of this may have to be met by the proposer, but some companies are prepared to write term assurances for a reasonable period up to quite substantial amounts with little medical evidence, provided that the proposer's age does not greatly exceed the usual age limits for non-medical underwriting.

There are two important variations of term assurance considered below.

Decreasing Term Assurance

This is an ordinary term assurance issued for a sum assured which decreases at specified intervals. It is commonly used in connection with loans that are repayable by instalments, e.g., a building society mortgage. In this type of transaction there is a reduction in the principal outstanding from time to time, and so a decreasing term assurance provides the cheapest way of covering the borrower for the amount he owes. This is illustrated in Chapter 9.

A level annual premium payable throughout the term of the policy cannot always be charged for this type of policy, because, if it were, the cost of the amount at risk in the early years might exceed the premiums charged, and if the policy lapsed the balance owing could not be recovered. To meet this difficulty, a higher premium is sometimes charged, payable for a period less than the full term of the policy. When the policy is used to cover a building society loan a single premium is sometimes charged. The amount advanced by the building society may then be correspondingly increased and the premium brought into the loan repayments.

Decreasing term assurance has another important use today, which is to cover estate duty liability on gifts not otherwise exempt if the donor dies within the statutory period of seven years. Since the proportion of the property on which duty is assessed decreases progressively after four, five and six complete years have elapsed from the date of the gift, a corresponding (or nearly corresponding) reduction is required in the assurance in force over these seven years. Policies designed specifically to cover this type of contingency are called gift protection policies, and one of these is illustrated in Plan XXXI.

Convertible Term Assurance

This is ordinary term assurance issued for a much longer period of years than is normal for this class of policy and containing an option to the effect that the policyholder can at any time convert it without evidence of health to a permanent contract, i.e., whole life or endowment assurance for the same or a smaller sum assured. If the option is not exercised the assurance lapses at the end of the original term. A policy with this provision is obviously of great value to someone who needs more life assurance cover than he could afford if it were wholly established on a permanent basis at outset. By taking part of it in this form, the cost is reduced without diminishing the prospect of permanency later. The premiums payable are comparatively moderate, being a little larger at young ages than the corresponding premiums for ordinary term assurance. But it is better to take out this type of assurance in conjunction with a permanent policy, and some companies offer a contract which combines convertible term with whole life or endowment assurance, the ratio of convertible term to whole life or endowment assurance being frequently about four to one. One or two companies writing policies on this basis make virtually no extra charge for the conversion option. Policies of this type are often given fancy names which have no particular significance.

Family Income Assurance

This type of policy also bears many different names and is frequently superimposed on whole life or endowment policies, or mixtures of both. Essentially, however, it is a decreasing term assurance which, instead of a capital sum, provides the value of that sum paid in instalments over the remainder of the period of assurance. It thus ensures a fixed annual income for a specified period and, since people normally measure the needs of their dependants in terms of income, it is often convenient to have life assurance written in this form as well. An example is where life assurance is required to cover the maintenance of school fees. The chief value of income insurance lies in the fact that it enables a husband to insure part of his earnings over the period when their loss would be most keenly felt and so concentrate the life assurance protection for his family in the years when it is most needed.

As a rule, the premium for income benefits unattached to a basic whole life or endowment policy is limited to about two-thirds of the full income period, but one or two companies allow the premiums to be spread over the entire period. The income period can nowadays be taken, if required, right up to the date when the life assured would have reached the age of 65 if he had lived.

The disadvantage implicit in any decreasing term assurance, that it is a wasting asset, resides equally, of course, in a policy where income is substituted for capital. For this reason it is normally unwise to have a large amount of insurance in this form. The occasion for family income assurance is when normal life assurance cover needs to be temporarily reinforced, usually when the family is growing up. It therefore goes well with whole life assurance, especially when this is equity-linked or participates in profits. Family income insurance can be written on the life of husband and wife to provide an income benefit on the death of either. The idea of insuring the life of his wife does not normally occur to a husband who typically regards himself as self-supporting, but it is worth considering. Since an income benefit is really a series of capital payments and is so expressed in the policy, it does not attract tax, which is a point in its favour. However, because the sums assured are capital the proposer should, unless the policy is written under the provisions of the Married Women's Property Act, specify in his will the persons to whom he wishes the benefit to be paid. He will normally intend the income benefit to be used for the maintenance and support of his family but in certain circumstances, in the absence of clear instructions in his will or if he dies intestate, this intention could be defeated.

Assurances on More than One Life

The types of life assurance dealt with above can be effected on more than one life to serve special purposes. Those chiefly used are as follows:

Joint Whole Life Assurance

Two or more lives can be assured and the sum assured is payable on the death of the first to die. When this happens, the contract is at an end. It is chiefly used by husband and wife where both stand to lose financially by the other's death and so protect themselves by arranging for the policy moneys to be payable to the survivor. It can also be used on the lives of partners, with the object of replacing capital that may be withdrawn on the death of a partner. Naturally, in this type of policy, the more lives that are assured the greater the premium.

Last Survivor Assurance

This is the same as above, except that the sum assured is payable on the death not of the first to die but of the last to die of the lives assured. This difference has the effect of *reducing* the premium the more lives that are assured. Last survivor assurance is sometimes of use in connection with leases granted during the lifetime of several people.

Joint Life Term Assurance

This is self-explanatory and may serve the same purpose as joint whole life assurance where assurance is required for a limited period only.

Contingent Assurance

This can sometimes take quite complicated forms, but basically it serves to protect a third party against the financial loss which might arise if one person who has an interest in surviving another dies first. Thus a trust may be drawn up which provides that Smith will be entitled to certain property on the death of Jones, provided that Smith is then living. Smith may then wish to protect his wife against the contingency that he predeceases Jones or, alternatively, some other third party may wish to protect himself against this contingency because he has purchased the interest from Smith. In either case, Smith would be known as the life assured and Jones as the counter-life, and if the counter-life dies first no claim arises and the contract comes to an end.

This type of assurance can be obtained by payment of a single premium or annual premiums.

Child's Deferred Assurance

This was once regarded as a useful way of giving a child a start in life with some capital and/or life assurance on ground floor terms. Up to the age of 21, the assurance is in effect a pure endowment with a full return of premiums, or the surrender value of the policy if this is greater on the death of the child. At the age of 21, when the child is able to give a legal discharge of a contract, he or she has the option of continuing the policy, at the same premium and without medical examination, as a whole life, or endowment assurance payable at a selected age. However, inflation has tended to rob this type of policy of any value, and since it does not qualify under Finance Act, 1968, it will probably disappear from the scene.

6

Primarily for Investment

Endowment Assurance

THIS IS the most popular form of assurance in this country at the present time. The sum assured is payable at the end of a chosen term, or at death if this occurs previously. Companies usually quote their rates for endowment assurance in two ways: for policies to mature (1) at specified ages and (2) at the end of a specified term of years. But, in practice, the first is a little misleading, because an endowment assurance almost invariably matures on an anniversary of its date of issue.

Because payment is made on survival, i.e., within a fixed period, endowment assurance provides less cover than whole life assurance for the same premium. Although, therefore, life assurance is an essential part of the contract, the long-term purpose of endowment assurance is personal saving. If the assurance matures at the end of a comparatively short term, the cost of the life assurance element may be very small indeed in relation to the balance required for the investment portion. Saving is, of course, a feature of whole life assurance as well, but in a less personal form.

It is interesting to consider those features of endowment assurance which distinguish it from other methods of personal saving.

First, the initial payment secures an interest in a much larger sum, contingent on the saver's death. Thus, from the start, a stronger issue than the need to save is brought to bear on the policyholder to encourage him to continue with his plan. Other savings systems today compete with endowment assurance in offering convenience of purchase, but none of them has so strong a compulsive element.

Secondly, provided the term is at least 10 years, income tax relief is allowed on part of each payment made. At the current standard rate of income tax, this means that up to 16½ per cent of the cost of the plan is being subsidized by the Exchequer. At present, this advantage is shared only with other cash contracts which have built-in life assurance.

Thirdly, the capital value of the contract is guaranteed and *so is the improvement in this provided by bonus additions.* The saver who puts his money in a unit trust may hope to gain more, but also bears the risk of loss.

Fourthly, when the investment matures the proceeds can be taken in different ways; for example, as a lump sum or in the form of a guaranteed income.

Fifthly, the proceeds on death or at maturity are not subject to capital gains tax.

There are, of course, other advantages of endowment assurance common to life assurance in general. For example, there is the automatic extension of time for payment. Without any interest charge the policyholder normally has a built-in contractual right to an extension of time for making payment (30 days) without loss of rights or privileges. When the policy has been in force for a little while, if the policyholder cannot meet his commitments, the company will usually be willing to lend him the premiums due against the security of the policy until such time as he is able to resume payment himself. The rate of interest charged for these loans is usually very reasonable. For a small extra premium a special clause can be added to the policy stipulating that payment will be kept up automatically if the policyholder falls permanently sick. And, finally, if all else fails, companies are normally willing to allow the policy to be reinstated within a reasonable period, subject where necessary to evidence of good health.

In other words, the person who chooses to save by endowment assurance can expect every possible privilege and help to enable him to complete his plan and secure the ultimate benefit of it to himself and his family.

What has been said underlines the value of endowment

assurance as a *method* of saving, encouraged by tax reliefs. There remains the important question of the return the endowment assurance saver may expect on his investment. Life assurance companies achieve widely different results on their with-profit policies, so that no common basis can be established either on present bonus estimates or past performance. Any figures quoted therefore will relate to the most competitive companies only. In calculating yield, it is possible to deduct the cost of the life assurance element and work out the rate of interest required to accumulate the cash sum and estimated bonuses at maturity with the balance of the premium deposit. In this way a common basis is established for comparing the yield on an endowment assurance with the return on other types of security where life assurance is absent. To do this, however, does injury to the nature of the contract, which owes part of its value as a method of saving to the fact that the whole of the sum being saved is paid at death. But, in making this type of calculation, full credit can be taken for tax relief.

The estimates given below are based on net premiums after deducting income tax rebate but not the cost of life assurance. The figures show the yield which would have been obtained on leading with-profit policies maturing in 1968 had the taxpayer secured the present standard rate tax relief (8*s* 3*d* in the £) through-

	Policy maturing in 1968		*Policy starting in 1969*	
	net yield (per cent)	*gross yield (per cent)*	*net yield (per cent)*	*gross yield (per cent)*
25-year term (male, 30 next birthday at entry)	7¼	12⅓	6¼	10½
15-year term (male, 45 next birthday at entry)	7½	12¾	6¼	10½

out, and the estimated yield on policies taken out in 1969 and maturing in the future on the same tax assumptions and assuming current rates of bonus used in quotations. These estimates may of course be wide of the mark, but are unlikely to be overstated as no account has been taken of special bonuses.

The equivalent net yields on non-profit policies effected at current rates would be, for the 25-year term $3\frac{3}{4}$ per cent, for the 15-year term $4\frac{1}{2}$ per cent. A with-profits policy is really a non-profit policy with an additional premium which secures the bonuses. On current bonus rates, the return on this additional premium might be as high as 14 per cent, net of tax.

A with-profits policy in a well-managed company will, in normal circumstances, always prove a better investment than a without-profits contract, and it is also generally true that a short-term endowment will, within certain limits, produce a better yield than a long-term policy. However, as no relief of income tax is allowed on any premiums in excess of 7 per cent of the sum assured, the best yield in any particular instance will generally be produced by a with-profits policy running for a term of years corresponding with an annual premium of this amount provided the term is at least 10 years so that the policy qualifies.

Judged from the investment standpoint, the performance of endowment assurance, excellent though it is, may nonetheless be thought disappointing when compared with the spectacular results that would have been achieved over corresponding periods in the past had the saver invested the same amounts in a good unit or investment trust. The past, however, is not a reliable guide here, for two reasons at least. First, the rapid growth in the value of equity shares since the war, which accounts for these results, is not likely to be repeated on the same scale again. At the beginning of the period, the average yield on the purchase price of good class equities was higher than that on gilt-edged. The position has now been reversed and the price of equities discounts to a much greater extent the prospects of future income growth. In other words, the time has been reached when fixed interest securities and ordinary shares (in both of which life funds have a stake) are probably a great deal more nearly in balance. The second reason why comparative estimates based on past results are invalid is that the improvement in the bonuses paid by companies over this period has been largely met out of income. So far, the reserves created by the improvement in capital values have been largely untapped, and therefore provide a present source of future profit, as well as giving strong backing to the maintenance of the current level of bonuses.

The continuing popularity of equity investment has, however, led more and more companies to introduce an alternative to the traditional endowment assurance, and these equity-linked contracts are discussed below. In general, they are more suitable for long-term investment.

Short-term endowment assurances are particularly valuable to provide for a child's educational or professional training (*see* Chapter 13). Over the longer term, they are used extensively for house purchase (Chapter 12). On the same principle, it is possible to buy shares with the help of a loan from an insurance company repayable by endowment assurance (Chapter 15). Endowment assurance coupled with a guaranteed annuity rate can be used in different ways to provide a retirement pension (Chapters 16 and 17).

Equity-linked Endowment Contracts

The idea of these is that the savings element of life assurance should be harnessed to unit and investment trusts or the performance of a special fund managed by the insurance company. Since the first edition of this book there has been a marked increase in the number of companies offering contracts in this form. The advantage they offer over straightforward investment in similar securities rests mainly on the fact that, at present, premiums qualify for the normal tax reliefs accorded to life assurance premiums. Thus the investor who pays tax at 8*s* 3*d* in the £ gets a reduction of 16½ per cent on the price of the units purchased, less the cost of the life assurance cover. For a man, e.g., under the age of 50 the life assurance cost will normally be less than 16½ per cent of the premium, so that he will obtain his units at a discount.

The essential difference between these contracts from the insurance point of view, as distinct from the difference in backing the unit trust to which the contracts are linked, is the nature and extent of the various guarantees of capital, interest and mortality. This is one set of considerations relevant to a comparison of these contracts with ordinary endowment assurance as a means of saving. To start with, none of the contracts, except for Type I below, is fully covered by a guaranteed minimum cash value, so that if the stock market is at the bottom of a slump at maturity the investor stands to lose some of the premiums he has paid. If the investor dies soon after starting his plan, this consideration is not very important because the bulk of the benefit his dependants receive will be in cash, anyway. At maturity, this particular risk is minimized in the case of those contracts which provide for units to be purchased by a fixed sum payable at regular intervals from start to finish. The reason for this is that, on the basis described, more units are bought when prices are low and fewer units when they are high. Thus the longer the policy runs the less likely it is that the average cost of the units will be higher than the price prevailing at any one time. This method of purchase is called 'low cost averaging'.

Taking into account these points, contracts can be roughly classified as follows:

Type I

This is an endowment assurance under which the sum assured is directly related to the price of, or actually payable in, the units of a designated trust. Since each premium is deemed to have been invested in these units at the time it is paid, the investor gets the benefit of low cost averaging. The company can actually invest the money where it thinks fit, but at maturity or death the investor gets the sum assured, plus any capital appreciation in the price of the units at that time over the average price he is deemed to have paid. If the price of the units is below this average he still gets the full sum assured. This type of contract can be with or without profits in the form of reversionary bonuses. An example of the former type is given in Chapter 15. The example chosen includes permanent sickness and accident cover as an optional extra.

Type II

This is on the lines of Type I above except that there is no guaranteed minimum. At maturity, the proceeds of the policy are payable partly in units and partly in cash. For example, if the investor died after two premiums had been bought out of a total of 15, the death benefit would be the units purchased by the two premiums plus a cash sum equal in amount to the 13 premiums remaining to be paid. The insurance company may guarantee in advance the amount of each premium which will be invested in the units, the balance covering the cost of the life assurance and its expenses. Since decreasing-term assurance is being used, some insurance companies protect themselves against early lapse of the policy by charging a larger amount of the premium to life assurance in the first years.

Under this type of contract, as with Type I above, the income from the units is retained by the company and interest is allowed to the policyholder in the premium calculations.

Type III

This differs from Types I and II chiefly because the income from the units purchased is re-invested to purchase further units for the policyholder. It is an endowment assurance without profits, in the sense that it does not participate in the profits of the insurance company. An endowment policy, say for 15 years, is taken out for an annual premium of £100. From each premium the company deducts a sum to cover the mortality risk and its expenses. The sum might be £8 for the first 11 years and £3 thereafter. The balance of the premium is invested in units of the particular trust (or shares of a special fund managed by the insurance company) and the net dividends on these units or shares are automatically re-invested as they fall due, so that the investor gets the extra benefit of the capital appreciation of these at the maturity of the policy. The benefit on death is the same as under Type II. In this case, the company's guarantee excludes both capital and interest, and is limited to the mortality risk and expenses. It is the closest of all to straightforward investment in a unit trust and, compared with such an investment, the only real difference is the tax relief on the premiums and a slight tax advantage on the treatment of the dividends.

An important variant of this type combines investment of 100 per cent of part of the premium in units with whole life assurance for the balance, thereby compelling the saver to insure his life on a permanent footing and providing a fully guaranteed sum assured on death and a guaranteed surrender value at maturity in respect of the life assurance element. This contract is illustrated in Chapter 15. This principle is extended in the case of equity-linked whole life assurance.

Other Considerations

More important than deciding which scheme devotes the largest proportion of contributions to the purchase of units is to choose the unit trust likely to give the best performance in the years ahead. This is because a relatively small increase in the rate of capital appreciation of the units will compensate for the biggest difference there is likely to be in the proportion of premium effectively allocated between the various schemes. Instead of a unit trust the underlying fund may be one managed by the insurance company, which calls for judgement on the investment expertise of the company in question. A further consideration is the question of capital gains tax raised by the Finance Act, 1965, and this is discussed in Chapter 15.

Pure Endowment

A pure endowment provides for payment of the sum assured at the end of a given term on survival only. In its strict form, there is no payment whatsoever if the life assured dies beforehand, though, normally, pure endowment policies are issued on the basis that the premiums are returned with or without interest on death.

Where premiums are forfeited in the event of death, the policy is the reverse of life assurance and clearly appeals only to those people who have a strong faith in their survival. It may be interesting to recount the case of a pure endowment policy issued a few years ago on the life of a man aged 70 for a sum of £22,000 payable on his survival to the age of 100. The single premium was only £500, so he had relatively little to lose. It is worth noting that when this type of policy is combined with term assurance it becomes a normal endowment assurance. No surrender values are allowed on the basis described and policies issued after 19th March 1968 do not qualify so that there is a surtax liability on survival.

7

Annuities

Jane Austen, through one of her characters, said that an annuity is a very serious business. She may have considered, as many others have since, the need for caution in a transaction which involves the surrender of capital. In return for the annuitant's capital, the insurance company undertakes to pay him or her an income for the rest of their life. The annuitant thus gets, in effect, a gradual repayment of this capital plus interest; but unless the annuity is guaranteed payable for a minimum period of years, the capital dies with the annuitant.

An annuity contract can thus be described as an assurance against outliving capital. If a person invests his capital at retirement and can live off the interest then he does not need this assurance. But if he has to draw on his capital to supplement the interest he risks living to the point at which his capital will be exhausted. Instead, the purchase of an annuity offers him the opportunity to pool his capital with that of others, so that the extra needed by those who live long is made up from that left over by those who die early.

For many people with limited capital resources this insurance arrangement is essential for self-protection or the protection of dependants. Even if the protection is not needed, an annuity may still prove to be an excellent investment for someone who wants to increase his spendable income. This is primarily because, where the annuity is privately purchased (*see* Chapter 3), only the portion representing interest is subject to tax. Consequently, for those who pay surtax, a relatively small investment of capital will produce a substantial increase in spendable income. The same result might be achieved by progressively drawing on capital, but much less conveniently.

Experience shows that annuitants as a class live longer than the average person. For a person with below average health an annuity may therefore be a bad bargain, unless he can satisfy the insurers that his expectation of life is reduced and obtain a correspondingly better rate. Experience also shows that on average women live longer than men, and for this reason women get a lower annuity rate.

Immediate Single Life Annuity

In return for the purchase price, the company undertakes to pay a guaranteed income for the remainder of life. The annuity is usually payable half-yearly in arrear, so that the first instalment is made six months after payment of the purchase money. If the annuity is paid in quarterly or monthly instalments, the cost is greater. The last instalment is normally the instalment due on the date which immediately precedes death, no further proportionate payment being made to cover the period from then up to the date of death. This is called an 'annuity curtate'. If a final proportionate payment is made, the annuity is said to be apportionable or complete.

No medical evidence is required for an annuity since it is tacitly assumed that anyone contemplating purchasing an annuity is in good health. But it is possible for someone whose health is impaired, and who is prepared to submit to medical examination at his own expense, to get favourable terms if the evidence shows that his life expectation is below normal.

In all cases, evidence of age is required at the time the proposal is made.

The following variations are available:

(*a*) The annuity is guaranteed payable for a fixed period and thereafter until death.

(*b*) Sufficient payments are guaranteed to cover the return of the purchase money (sometimes called a capital protected annuity).

(*c*) Provision is made for the return of a portion of the purchase money, e.g., one-half, if death occurs within a defined period, say, five years.

Any one of these guarantees increases the cost of the annuity. Similar guarantees are available in most of the other types of annuity described below.

Immediate annuity rates are subject to frequent changes dependent on current investment conditions. For this reason they cannot normally be guaranteed more than a month or two from the time a quotation is given. The best time for purchasing an immediate annuity is usually when capital is generally short and interest rates high. From time to time, however, exceptionally favourable terms can be obtained independently of these market conditions from certain companies. These instances usually arise when a company wants to attract capital to balance the tax position on its annuity fund, and as soon as this limited objective has been achieved the rates are withdrawn.

For these and other reasons the annuity market is one which calls for very special study and anyone who purchases an annuity without first consulting a good life assurance broker is being remarkably foolish.

The following sample annuity rates show approximate differences in the amounts of annuity that can be bought at various ages and the corresponding tax free portions, but for the reasons given above they are not an accurate guide to the rates normally current.

SPECIMEN ANNUITIES FOR £100 PURCHASE PRICE

MALE			FEMALE		
Age at purchase	*Gross annuity*	*Tax free*	*Age at purchase*	*Gross annuity*	*Tax free*
	£ *s* *d*	£ *s* *d*		£ *s* *d*	£ *s* *d*
50	9 8 1	3 17 3	50	8 18 0	3 6 8
60	11 3 5	5 12 6	60	10 3 4	4 13 5
65	12 13 0	7 0 11	65	11 4 10	5 14 8
70	14 15 7	9 1 5	70	12 16 2	7 4 9
75	17 16 11	11 19 6	75	15 2 0	9 8 3
80	22 5 5	16 4 0	80	18 9 10	12 12 6

Immediate Annuity More than One Life

It is possible to effect immediate annuities on two or more lives. There are broadly two types:

(*a*) Joint Life: The annuity ceases at the death of the first to die.

(*b*) Joint Life and Survivor: The annuity continues until the death of the survivor. A variation of this provides for the annuity to be reduced on the first death. For example, a husband and wife may purchase an annuity of £500 per annum while they are both alive, reducing to £350 when only one of them is alive.

When an annuity is purchased on two or more lives, the question of estate duty arises and it may be better to achieve the required result by purchasing two separate annuities, (*i*) a single life annuity, and (*ii*) a reversionary annuity. The present tax and estate duty position is summarized later in this chapter.

Temporary Annuity

The annuity payments cease at the end of a selected period or at previous death. At first sight this seems rather a waste of money, as no permanent income is provided in return for the capital given up. But if the capital is replaced at the end of the term the proposition becomes much more interesting. This can be achieved by taking out, in conjunction with the temporary annuity, an endowment or equity-linked with-profits policy for a similar term. The premiums for the endowment policy, which of course attract tax relief, can be met from the annuity payments and the proceeds of the policy can be re-invested at maturity to purchase an annuity for the remainder of life. This is a good arrangement for someone who contemplates buying an annuity at a relatively young age, as the initial commitment is limited in duration and the bonuses on the endowment policy provide the capital appreciation required to restore the purchasing power of the amount invested in the annuity. An example of how this works is given in Chapter 19.

Deferred Annuity

The annuity is not paid immediately the transaction is made

but at a specified later date. It can be purchased by a single premium, or the cost can be spread over the period of deferment by level annual premiums. In either event, the cost is less than that of an immediate annuity since it allows for interest earned by the company over the period of deferment. If death occurs before the annuity vests, the premiums are usually returned without interest or with interest at a moderate rate. If the return on death excludes interest, the cost is less. Just before payment of the annuity commences, it is customary to allow the annuitant the option of a cash payment instead.

A drawback to this type of contract is that no tax relief is allowed on the premiums unless the contract is one making approved pension provision, e.g., under S.22 and 23 of the Finance Act, 1956. The special contracts available for the self-employed and others under this Act are described later. For someone who is ineligible for these it is normally better to take out an endowment policy and apply the policy moneys at maturity to purchase an immediate annuity (*see* Chapter 16).

Reversionary Annuity

In its simplest form a reversionary annuity provides that payments commence at the time one person (the nominee) survives another and then continue until the nominee's death. If the nominee dies first the contract comes to an end and the premium or premiums paid are forfeited. The person on whose life the annuity depends usually has to be medically examined, but this can be avoided if he simultaneously takes out an immediate annuity on his own life, since if death occurs early the profit to the insurance company on the immediate annuity will roughly cover the loss arising from early payment of the reversionary annuity.

This form of annuity is particularly suitable for a husband wishing to provide a fixed income for his wife after his death, and when it is coupled with an immediate annuity on the husband's life the same object is achieved as under a joint life and survivor annuity described above, but with important tax and estate duty differences.

No surrender values are allowed for a reversionary annuity.

Notes on Estate Duty on Annuities
(*see also* Chapter 4)

Annuity bought by Annuitant

If 'A' effects an annuity on his own life for his own benefit, ceasing on his death, no estate duty liability can arise on 'A's' death.

If the annuity is payable for a guaranteed period and thereafter for life, and the annuitant dies during the guaranteed period, duty is payable on the commuted value of all the outstanding instalments.

Annuity bought by Annuitant with a Gift of Money

If 'A' wishes to provide 'B' with an immediate annuity and gives 'B' the purchase money, the transaction is then regarded as a gift of cash, and if 'A' dies within seven years of the gift duty is payable on the cash sum (which is fully aggregable), subject to the graduated relief if 'A' survives the gift by more than four years.

Purchaser buys Annuity as a Gift to Annuitant

When the purchaser wishes to make a gift of an immediate annuity, it is possible for him to do so as trustee for, and on behalf of, the annuitant so that the annuitant is the beneficial owner of the annuity in terms of the policy and the policy is issued in the annuitant's name. Some companies have special proposal forms to suit this arrangement.

When a policy is issued in this manner, it is understood that under present law and practice no estate duty is payable if the purchaser dies after more than seven years from the date of purchase, with partial exemption after four years. As a result of Finance Act, 1968, where duty is payable the value of the annuity would be aggregated with the free estate.

Joint Life and Survivor Annuities

The estate duty position under a joint life and survivor annuity depends upon a number of factors, including the source of the purchase money, the manner in which the policy is written, and in some cases the ages of the annuitants.

(*a*) *Purchase price provided by both annuitants* (e.g., husband and wife)

The simplest example is where husband and wife each provide exactly one-half of the purchase price, they are of about the same age and they enjoy the annuity equally. It is understood that in this case no estate duty is payable on the first death, on the grounds that the beneficial interest which arises by survivorship was not purchased or provided by the deceased.

(*b*) *Purchase price provided by one of the annuitants* (e.g., husband)

Very often, where provision is required for husband and wife, the whole of the purchase price is found by the husband. If this is substantial and the question of estate duty important, it may be better for the husband to take out two policies as follows:

(i) An immediate annuity for himself; and
(ii) a reversionary annuity for his wife commencing on his death.

On this basis, should the husband die during the first five years, duty would be payable only on the value of the second annuity at the time of the husband's death. This would be treated as a gift, so that if he died after seven years, no duty would be payable. No duty would be payable on the wife's death in respect of either annuity.

As an alternative, the husband could give his wife the premium to buy her own annuity. The advantage of dealing with the matter in this way is that the duty liability is established at outset, subject only to legislative changes, and can be covered by a gift protection policy (*see* Plan XXXII).

(*c*) *Income tax (capital content)*

Under an ordinary joint life and survivor policy the capital content is determined at the outset and is a constant proportion of the annuity throughout. Where, however, two separate policies are issued, as in (*b*) above, the tax position is as follows:

(*i*) Husband's annuity: The capital content is determined at the outset. It is usually larger than the capital content on the joint life and survivor annuity. The amount of annuity liable to tax during the lifetime of the husband is thus reduced.

(*ii*) Widow's annuity: The capital content of this annuity depends on the age of the wife at the time of the husband's death and cannot, therefore, be determined at outset. Should the husband die soon after the annuities are purchased, the capital content may be considerably less than the capital content of the joint life and survivor annuities, so that more tax is payable.

Small Annuities

S.15 of the Finance Act, 1894, exempts certain small annuities from duty. Thus, if a person buys a joint life and survivor annuity (payable to himself and another) or a reversionary annuity (payable to another on his death) then, provided the annuity does not exceed £52, duty is not payable on his death. Only one such annuity is entitled to this exemption.

The exemption was extended by S.2 of the Finance Act, 1935, to provide that an annuity of less than £104 per annum which would, apart from its amount, be exempt, shall be treated for duty as if it were an annuity for twice its excess over £52. An annuity of £60 would, for example, be dutiable as an annuity of £16.

Equity-linked Annuities

The weakness of an annuity is that while it guarantees an income of a given amount it does not guard the purchasing power of that income. Enough publicity has been given to the plight of old age pensioners and others living on fixed incomes to make everyone aware of this shortcoming. An attempt has been made to overcome it by equating annuity benefits with the general level of share prices. The problem, however, is not as easy to solve as it is with endowment policies. This is because the benefits of the contract are not accumulating for payment in the future but are being released in the present. Naturally, an annuitant does not want to accept violent fluctuations in his income from year to year. Moreover, it is difficult in the case of a purchased life annuity to achieve on this basis a fair and workable system for calculating the capital element that is exempt from tax. In any event, until the gap between equity and fixed interest yields narrows, a competitive price for equity-linked immediate annuities cannot be offered. Deferred annuities are a different matter, and these are considered below.

Equity-linked Deferred Annuities for Self-employed

These cover annuities issued under S.22 and 23 of the Finance Act, 1956, which are discussed further in Chapter 16, with examples in Chapter 18. There are basically two types;

Type I.—The benefit is geared to the value of the units of a designated unit trust by means of an index, in much the same way as the equity-linked endowment policy of Type II described in Chapter 6. In this case, however, the benefits under the contract are secured by a series of single premiums and the index operates on the annuity benefit which each single premium purchases.

Type II.—In this case the company maintains a special variable annuity fund. The terms of the policy provide for a variable rate of accumulation during the period of deferment and, when the annuity vests, the option to take the amount accumulated to the credit of the policyholder either in the form of a fixed annuity, or as a variable annuity. In either event, the amount he receives will depend, first, on the number of accumulation units to his credit as determined by the value of the unit at the time each single premium is paid and, second, on their equivalent value in terms of annuity units, as determined by age, sex and type of annuity.

In general, Type II offers more protection to the annuitant than Type I, because the value of the benefits depends on the experience of a fund, the investment of which is wholly and exclusively in the hands of the company issuing the annuity policies, and the company can be expected to manage its fund to suit the special requirements of this class of business.

All equity-linked contracts are, of course, exposed to the danger that the policyholders' expectations can be sadly upset by economic, financial or fiscal action, but the upset would be most serious for annuitants.

Part Three

SUGGESTED PLANS

PART TWO described the chief classes of assurance and their uses. This part illustrates how these policies can be applied in given circumstances to achieve certain results.

In the case of with-profit policies it has been assumed, unless otherwise stated, that bonuses will be declared throughout the period of the assurance at either 70*s* per cent per annum simple or 60*s* per cent per annum compounded triennially, depending on the duration of cover. *In the light of recent declarations (such as 80s compound, plus special bonuses) these estimates must be regarded as definitely conservative and more likely to be exceeded than otherwise.* The underlying rates of premium are based on a selection of those currently used by leading companies.

The immediate annuity rates used are based on average rates over the period 1965 to 1968, and are well below the 1968 level. Current rates are, however, at historically high levels and it would be unwise to project them too far ahead. *Apart from the possibility of a fall in interest, it should be recognized that continuing improvement in life expectation will also have an adverse effect on rates in the long term.*

It has been assumed throughout that the standard rate of income tax will be maintained at 8*s* 3*d* in the £ and that sufficient tax is paid at this rate to cover the premiums qualifying for life assurance tax relief. Where the plan involves borrowing, it has similarly been assumed that the borrower is able to set off the whole of the interest charge against income taxable at this rate.

The plans are divided into three sections broadly corresponding to the classification of the policies described in Part Two.

Section I—Primarily for Protection

8 First Priorities

9 Family Security

8

First Priorities

PLAN I

A young man with no present dependants and in good health wants to secure permanent life assurance cover which is likely to maintain its real value in the future.

He takes out a whole life policy with profits, the premiums being payable throughout life. He resists the temptation to take out a non-profit policy, recognizing that if £3,000 is sufficient today the cover required in ten years' time might be one-third as much again. Assuming that the protection has not been called upon, by the age of 65, when he retires, the policy can then be made paid-up so that he is relieved of further premiums. When this happens, only the basic sum assured will be reduced, the accumulated bonuses remaining intact. Moreover, after the policy has been made paid-up it will continue to attract future bonus additions. The claim values in the example are the estimated amounts payable if death occurs at the ages stated. If at any time life assurance protection is no longer needed, the policy can be surrendered for a cash sum, and estimates of these cash values are included in the example.

Policy Description: Chapter 5

WHOLE LIFE ASSURANCE WITH PROFITS

Male, aged 21 next birthday

BENEFITS:

Sum assured payable on death	£3,000 0*s* 0*d*
Bonuses will be added to this sum	

COST:

Yearly premium	£60 0s 0d
Income tax saving	9 18 0
Net annual cost	£50 2s 0d

Estimated Claim Value

Assuming that bonuses accumulate at the rate of 60*s* per cent per annum compounded triennially, the amount payable in the event of death will be:

If death occurs after 20 years	£5,334
30 years	7,101
40 years	9,474
50 years	12,624

Specimen Surrender Values (on above assumption)

Number of full years premiums paid and years in force

30	£3,000
45	£7,500

Specimen Paid-up Value (on above assumption)

Number of full years premiums paid and years in force

45	£10,250

On conversion to a paid-up assurance the policy illustrated will continue to participate in the profits of the company. If, therefore, premiums are discontinued after the age of 65, the policy will give life assurance cover of £10,250 plus future bonus additions on this sum.

PLAN II

A young man with a wife and young child to protect needs twice as much cover at outset than can be afforded at present under Plan I. He could supplement by temporary assurance, but if he does this he takes a risk that his health might subsequently deteriorate when the opportunity of getting permanent cover on equally good terms would be lost.

The solution to this problem is to combine convertible term

assurance with Plan I. This provides a combination of permanent and temporary cover at a cost per £100 sum assured below that of Plan I, with the advantage that the temporary cover can be made permanent at any time in the next 15 years without any evidence of health at the date of conversion.

Policy Description: Chapter 5

WHOLE LIFE ASSURANCE WITH PROFITS PLUS CONVERTIBLE TERM ASSURANCE

Male, aged 21 next birthday

BENEFITS:

Sum assured payable on death	
(*a*) Whole life	£2,000 0*s* 0*d*
Bonuses will be added to this sum	
(*b*) Term assurance (ceasing after 15 years)	4,000 0 0
	£6,000 0*s* 0*d*

COST:

Yearly premium	£49 8*s* 0*d*
Income tax saving	8 3 0
Net annual cost	£41 5*s* 0*d*

Conversion Option

At any time during the first 15 years the term assurance can be converted in whole or in part to whole life assurance (or endowment assurance) without evidence of health at the date of conversion. If this option is exercised by converting the full amount to whole life assurance with profits at the end of the period, the adjusted cost would then be:

Yearly premiun	£152 0*s* 0*d*
Income tax saving	25 2 0
	£126 18*s* 0*d*

Assuming that the original whole of life assurance had earned bonuses at the rate of 60*s* per cent compounded triennially, the total assurance in force when this option is exercised would then be £7,078. Thereafter bonuses would be added to this total sum.

9

Family Security

PLAN III

A married man aged 40 (wife aged 35) has three children, aged 5, 3 and 1. His assets consist of a policy covering the mortgage on his house, and a whole life with profits, with a current claim value of £5,000.

The purpose of this plan is to provide supplementary cover for a limited period while the children are growing up and the loss of the husband's income on his death would be most keenly felt. It is designed to leave the major part of the capital sum intact so that it can be invested to produce a current income from interest and, at a later date, re-invested in an annuity for life.

Assuming that the interest on this sum would amount to £250 a year, it is estimated that an additional £200 a year will be needed for each child until the youngest reaches, say, the age of 21. In the event of the husband's death, the plan provides a guaranteed income benefit of £600 a year for 20 years. While he lives, it also gives him the option of changing the major part of this benefit to a permanent form of assurance. It is reasonable to assume that by the time the income benefit ceases the wife will have taken a job and be earning enough to support herself until she retires at the age of 60. At that time, the proceeds of the whole life policy can be re-invested to purchase an annuity payable at the rate of about £9 per £100 purchase price.

As explained in Chapter 5, the income benefit is expressed in the policy as instalments of capital and is not subject to income tax.

Policy Description: Chapter 5

FAMILY INCOME BENEFITS

Male, aged 40 next birthday

BENEFITS:

In the event of death within 20 years a tax-free income for the remainder of such period at the rate of	£600 0s 0d per annum

COST:

Yearly premium (payable for 20 years)	£28 5s 0d
Income tax saving	4 13 0
Net annual cost	£23 12s 0d

Conversion Option

At any time during the currency of the policy it can be converted into a whole life or endowment assurance for a sum assured amounting to 75 per cent of the balance of the income benefit remaining. For example, after the policy had been in force five years it could be changed to a whole life assurance, with profits, for £6,750, without any evidence of health. The revised yearly premium would then be £245 10s 0d.

Note: A reduction in the premium rate (say 10s = per £100 income benefit) is normally given if the policy is added to a whole of life or endowment policy.

PLAN IV

A disadvantage of straight family income benefit is that it provides no hedge against inflation. This is the chief reason why it is so important to associate with it a substantial capital sum which accumulates by the addition of bonuses while the assurance remains in force and can be re-invested to go on growing when the life assured dies. But it is possible to have family income benefits participating in profits as well.

The plan illustrated below is on the same basis as Plan III, except that a higher premium can be afforded for the immediate cover required which is set up on a profit sharing basis.

Policy Description: Chapter 5

FAMILY INCOME BENEFITS WITH PROFITS

Male, aged 40 next birthday

BENEFITS:

In the event of death within 20 years a tax-free income for the remainder of such period at the rate of	£600 0*s* 0*d* per annum *plus profits*

Under the contract illustrated bonuses are linked to those arising under pension contracts, and the rate of bonus applicable when the contract was first introduced was £3 10*s* per annum compound. Accordingly, in calculating the figures shown below this rate has been substituted for the normal basis of 60*s* compounded triennially used for other illustrations in this book.

Thus at the beginning of the 11th year the benefit will have risen to £846 0*s* 0*d* per annum and in the 20th year will reach £1,152 0*s* 0*d*. It should be noted that bonuses accrue while the insurance company is on risk as well as when benefit is being paid out.

COST:

Yearly premium (payable for 20 years)	£36 4*s* 0*d*
Income tax saving	5 19 6
Net annual cost	£30 4*s* 6*d*

PLAN V

A young man, aged 30, has bought a house with the help of a mortgage from a building society. The mortgage is for £3,500, repayable in instalments of capital and interest over 25 years. He needs to cover the loan outstanding from year to year. As he already has sufficient life assurance in force to cover his other needs he requires this minimum protection only.

The building society may not require the loan to be covered by life insurance but it would be foolish of the borrower to neglect this precaution. The plan illustrated below provides decreasing term assurance sufficient to cover the debt outstanding from year to year if interest is charged up to 7 per cent.

Policy Description: Chapter 5

MORTGAGE PROTECTION AT MINIMUM COST

Male, aged 30 next birthday

Building Society Mortgage

Amount of loan outstanding	£3,500
Repayment term (or balance of original term)	25 years
Rate of interest not exceeding	7 per cent

BENEFITS:

In the event of death during the stated term, a sum sufficient to repay the balance of the loan (excluding any arrears) then outstanding under the mortgage

COST:

Yearly premium	£7	5s	0d
Income tax saving	1	4	0
Net annual cost	£6	1s	0d

PLAN VI

Although Plan V gives sufficient cover to extinguish the debt on the house in the event of death, it is wiser where possible to secure part of the required assurance on a permanent with-profits basis. This plan

provides the first £1,000 cover in the form of whole life assurance with profits and the balance by decreasing term assurance.

Policy Description: Chapter 5

MORTGAGE PROTECTION INCLUDING WHOLE LIFE ASSURANCE WITH PROFITS

Male, aged 30 next birthday

Building Society Mortgage

Amount of loan outstanding	£3,500
Repayment term (or balance of original term)	25 years
Rate of interest not exceeding	7 per cent

BENEFITS:

(1) In the event of death during the stated term a sum sufficient to repay the balance of the loan (excluding any arrears) then outstanding under the mortgage, subject to a minimum of	£1,000	plus bonuses on this sum
(2) On survival to the end of the mortgage period the policyholder will continue to be covered for £1,000 plus bonuses for the rest of his life on payment of the reduced premiums shown below. Estimated claim value at end of mortgage period	£2,052	

COST:

For first 20 years

Yearly premium	£32 7s 6d
Income tax saving	5 6 6
Net annual cost	£27 1s 0d

For next 5 years and life thereafter

Yearly premium	£28 0s 0d
Income tax saving	4 12 0
Net annual cost	£23 8s 0d

Surrender Option

At the end of the mortgage period the policy need not be maintained. If it is discontinued, the final sum assured and bonuses could be surrendered for approximately £800.

10

Permanent Sickness Insurance

THE MAIN object of life assurance is to cover a financial liability, but this does not only arise on death. For the self-employed man especially, and for others to a lesser degree depending on the provisions of their employment, there is a financial risk associated with prolonged sickness. Insuring one's health is not life assurance and by definition therefore falls outside the scope of this book. But in the form in which sickness *insurance* is permanent and non-cancellable it is closely related to life *assurance*, and the broad purposes that life assurance serve. It also happens to be business which *is* transacted by companies that only transact ordinary life assurances, as well as by general insurance or composite companies, and can be added to life policies.

The self-employed man is particularly vulnerable if he cannot work through illness or accident. A short illness may not make much difference. Prolonged inaction nearly always will. The sickness benefit under national insurance is a help but does not replace more than a small portion of normal earnings. So private sickness insurance is something worth considering in conjunction with other plans for family protection.

For real protection against sickness and accident a policy is needed that *cannot be cancelled by the insurance company on account of long or frequent claims.* Most sickness and accident insurances are, like most forms of general insurances, e.g., fire and motor, technically 'annual contracts', which means that when you pay a premium the company insures you for a year, but is under no obligation to insure you again at the end of the year. *Permanent* sickness insurance is different. A person who is healthy now and has a good medical history can insure against sickness and accident right up to retirement age and have no fear that cover will be withdrawn just at the time when it is needed most.

It is not sensible to cover short illnesses as the cost of doing so would be prohibitive. So a suitable period has to be chosen at the end of which, if illness continues, the benefit becomes payable. This is known as the period of deferment. It may be as short as say four weeks, or as long as two years. Naturally, the longer the period of deferment the lower the cost of cover.

The benefit under a permanent sickness (or permanent disability as it is sometimes called) policy can be expressed as a weekly or monthly sum, but may be calculated on a day-to-day basis, and covers Sundays and holidays as well as normal working days. *At present it is the practice of the Inland Revenue not to assess benefit for income tax until the claimant has received it continuously for a full fiscal year.*

It is normal for the insurance company to impose a ceiling on the benefit which, together with national insurance sickness benefit, will be, say, three-quarters of normal weekly or monthly earnings.

Before taking out this type of policy it is worth checking very carefully with the company or broker the circumstances in which benefit is payable. For example, one or two companies which specialize in this type of business stipulate only that the insured must be completely prevented by illness or accident from following *his own ordinary occupation.* They are not concerned as to whether the claimant might be capable of doing some other kind of work unless he voluntarily does so, in which case benefit does not cease but is payable at a rate scaled down to the loss of earnings. The modified benefit is such that the insured person is given some encouragement to turn to alternative work without feeling under any obligation to do so. Not all companies deal with the matter so generously.

PLAN VII

A professional man, aged 35 with two children, earns £2,500 a year. He has a substantial life policy with profits which, if maintained, is expected to yield an income of £1,500 on retirement at age 65. This is supplemented with whole life assurance and family income benefit sufficient to ensure an income to his dependants of £1,000 a year in the event of death. The total cost of these policies is £314 a year. He wants to provide in the event of prolonged sickness sufficient to meet the cost of these premiums and an income of £1,000 a year to live on.

PERMANENT SICKNESS INSURANCE

Total annual income required in the event of prolonged sickness	£1,314
Less National Insurance Sickness Benefit	488
Net amount per annum to be provided by permanent sickness insurance	£826

The annual cost of sickness benefit of £16 a week is	
if payment is deferred 13 weeks	£21 2*s* 8*d*
if payment is deferred 26 weeks	17 9 4
if payment is deferred 52 weeks	14 0 0

(If premiums are paid quarterly, the extra charge is 2½ per cent.)

While the benefit is being paid premiums are waived

If a claim is made, the full amount of benefit payable is £16 a week. But supposing that, after a while, the claimant took up alternative work earning £500 a year. He has lost four-fifths of his normal income, so he gets four-fifths of his benefit, i.e., £12 16*s* 0*d* per week.

An alternative method of providing permanent sickness cover in conjunction with savings and retirement plans is illustrated in Plans VIII and XXI.

II

Business and Partnership Risks

A BUSINESS may need protection against the loss of key employees, and it may be necessary to ensure that in the case of close companies and partnerships, that adequate provision is made to pay estate duty if the business is to continue on the deaths of the principals. In this chapter the use of life assurance is considered in relation to the special problems which arise in relation to key employees, partners and controlling directors.

Key Man Insurance

Sometimes the success of a business hinges very much on the efforts of one man who would be difficult to replace. In this situation there is a good case for taking out an insurance policy on his life for a sum calculated to cover the financial loss the business will suffer on his death. This precaution may also produce a good impression on creditors and shareholders.

The company takes out a policy of a suitable type depending on whether the risk period is short or long. If the employee concerned is engaged for a short time on important research a term assurance will be sufficient. If his appointment is permanent, a whole life policy will be needed. In the normal way, the premiums paid by the company will be allowable for tax as a legitimate business expense if it is accepted that the proceeds of the policy, should a claim arise, are treated as a trading receipt.

Partnership Assurance

The normal partnership deed will provide that, on the death of a partner, the surviving partner or partners acquires the deceased partner's share. There may also be a clause stating the valuation of the practice, such as one and a half or two years' profits, based on the average of the last three years. If there is no formal agreement constituting the partnership, or if the agreement is silent on this matter, then when a partner dies the partnership is immediately dissolved, unless agreement can be reached with the deceased partner's executors to buy his share for cash. It follows that however formally or informally a partnership is created, ready cash will be needed at an unknown future date or dates if the practice is to be kept intact. The only way of ensuring that the right funds are available *whenever* they are called for is through life insurance. To be specific, each partner's life must be insured for the value of his share.

Next to this fundamental need to safeguard the business on a partner's death there is the problem of providing for retirement. This point is frequently overlooked in partnership assurance plans but has a special bearing on the merits of the plan advocated here.

Before explaining this it is worth establishing five criteria for a good plan. They are as follows:

(1) Money in the right hands.
(2) Equitable division of cost.
(3) Maximum income tax relief.
(4) Minimum estate duty liability.
(5) Simplicity and flexibility.

At first sight, it appears that to achieve (1), (2) and (4) it is essential to adopt a scheme whereby the partners join together in insuring the lives of each other, and this is, in fact, the scheme most commonly put forward. For example, take a three-man partnership in which, for the sake of simplifying the example, the partners, A, B and C, have equal shares of £5,000 each. A and B therefore insure the life of C for £5,000 with which to purchase C's share, B and C do likewise with A, and so on. Money is in the right hands, the cost is divided equitably because each pays the premium for the benefit he receives, and there is no immediate estate duty liability since the policies are from the beginning the property of the beneficiaries. But there are two immediate disadvantages. First, the premiums do not attract income tax relief because they are on the life of another. Secondly, if there are many partners the insurance arrangements are complicated and become very difficult to adjust each time a new partner is taken on. As it is essential to the success of the scheme that premiums are maintained and that the policies remain free from encumbrances, some alteration to the partnership agreement is necessary, e.g., to provide that the premiums will be paid by the practice and debited to the partners' accounts.

Another way of achieving broadly the same object is for each partner to insure his own life and assign the policy to his partner(s). In this case the partners will not be paying premiums corresponding to the benefits they will receive and any inequalities must be ironed out by adjusting the terms of the partnership agreement. In addition, title to the policies has to be changed every time a new partner is taken on. If the policies qualify the premiums will rank for income tax relief. On the other hand, the policy moneys are likely to be dutiable under S.34 of the Finance Act, 1959 (*see* Chapter 4). More important, they will also now be liable for capital gains tax because the policies have been assigned for value. This method is therefore no longer practicable.

Implicit in both these plans is the idea that money in the right hands means money in the hands of the surviving partners. But looking beyond this immediate goal, the ultimate destination of these moneys is the deceased partner's estate. An important and separate problem, therefore, is the need to provide for payment of estate duty on the deceased partner's share in the partnership at the time of his death, which may otherwise fall on his widow or other dependants.

In view of the above, there is much to be said for approaching the problem of partnership assurance on the lines that, subject to suitable alterations to the partnership agreement, each partner is made individually responsible for providing the necessary funds for his dependants and for his retirement as well. The plan illustrated below is based on this approach. Its chief merit is that a partnership agreement is more flexible than an insurance policy, and where there are more than, say, two partners it is usually easier to cover future changes by adjusting the former than the latter.

PLAN VIII

It is assumed that there are four male partners who are all married and that the ages and percentage interests of these partners are:

	Age next birthday	*Percentage interest in partnership*
A.	55	35
B.	55	35
C.	40	20
D.	30	10

They are all to retire at the age of 65 and will require to be paid on retirement or earlier death, A and B £7,000: C £4,000 and D £2,000.

The immediate and most serious problem is the provision of funds for A and B upon their retirement or earlier death. If no advance provision is made, the remaining partners would be faced (unless they had the good fortune to find new partners with sufficient capital resources) with the necessity of supporting the retiring or deceased partner(s) or their families out of current income of the partnership, in addition to paying salaries to new assistants to take over their work.

The solution lies in spreading as much as possible of this liability over the years prior to their retirement and, simultaneously, making provision for a part of the capital required in the event of premature death.

In the case of the two younger partners it should be possible to make the necessary provision in full, as well as allowing for a future increase in the value of their shares.

Appropriate provision would be made by each partner taking out an endowment assurance with-profits policy on his life under the provisions of the Married Women's Property Act for the absolute benefit of wife or children. A and B might take out policies for a sum assured of £5,000 to cover the major part of the liability, and C and D policies for sums assured of £4,000 and £2,000, respectively. In the case of A and B, the policy moneys would be taken into account in arriving at the net amounts they are entitled to receive in respect of their interest in the partnership. In the case of C and D, the agreement would be altered to provide that the benefit of the partnership passed to the surviving partners free of any obligation to make payments to them or to their estates on retirement or death.

So far the plan succeeds in satisfying four of the five criteria listed above, namely, money in the right hands, maximum income tax relief, minimum estate duty liability and simplicity. The estate duty saving arises because, if £5,000 were paid to the estate of A in respect of his share, this sum would be fully dutiable. Under the plan, each partner is able to take advantage of 'normal' expenditure exemption to convey his share free or largely free of estate duty. The remaining criterion, equitable division of cost, is not implicit in the plan and has to be achieved by including in the modifications made to the partnership agreement such provisions as will compensate the partners for the costs of the plan in proportion to their true liabilities, i.e., to provide the sums required on the death or retirement of the other partners and not their own.

Policy Description: Chapter 6

PARTNERSHIP ASSURANCE BY ENDOWMENT ASSURANCE WITH PROFITS

Male partner	*Age next birthday*	*Basic sum assured* (£)	*Estimated value at retirement at age of 65* (£)	*Gross premiums* (£)	*Tax relief* (£)	*Net cost* (£)
A	55	5,000	6,670	562	58	504
B	55	5,000	6,670	562	58	504
C	40	4,000	8,208	181	30	151
D	30	2,000	5,470	64	11	53

It will be noted that, in the case of C and D, the policies cover not only their present shares but a future increase in their value.

In order to obtain maximum tax relief, and to do broad justice between the partners, it is suggested that the partnership agreement be modified to provide that the first £1,787 of profits be divided as follows:

A	£743
B	£743
C	£222
D	£79

and that the balance of the profits be divided in the usual proportions of 35, 35, 20 and 10 per cent This calculation takes into account the net tax payable on the profits so divided, so that each partner is able to bear his own premium without loss (on the assumption that no partner is subject to surtax on his earned income).

So far we have dealt with two of the three major possible contingencies which will undoubtedly occur in a partnership; the third is inability to carry on work either completely or only partially, because of sickness or accident. It is inevitable that a partner will either (*a*) retire, (*b*) die, or (*c*) be disabled, and if the latter happens the remaining partners may have to pay someone to take over the disabled partner's work. There is one insurance company which will cover disability at no extra initial premium. Since disability insurance is not by itself eligible for tax relief, this can be a great advantage. The cost of meeting the disability claims is taken from the bonuses of the with-profits policyholders as a group. Thus the cost is met in a relatively painless way, is based on actual experience and is likely for that reason to be lower than the amount that would have to be charged if this took the normal form of a fixed addition to the premiums.

To take our partnership position:

A and B have left it too late in their lives to obtain this benefit; C, in the event of being sick or disabled for three months or longer, would receive to the age of 60, £624 0*s* 0*d* per annum.

plus waiver of his premium; D would receive £312 0*s* 0*d* per annum, plus waiver of his premium.

These benefits are calculated at £3 per week for each £1,000 basic sum assured under the policy. Benefit is paid up to the age of 60, but, if payment is deferred for six months, payments would continue up to the age of 65. In addition, each partner would receive the maturity value of his endowment policy.

The bonuses received by C and D at maturity would clearly be lower than under the normal plan shown above, since the cost of meeting disability claims for all policyholders as a group is deducted before calculating bonuses on this class of policy, and it is not possible at this stage to estimate the difference in the bonus. Incidentally, the premium rates of the company offering this special contract are actually about 7 per cent lower than those used in the example.

Life Assurance for Controlling Directors

Controlling directors of 'close companies' are unable to participate in the conventional pension scheme and provision for their dependants has normally to be met from net taxed income. Moreover, the restrictive legislation governing 'close companies' entails enforced distributions which suffer income tax and surtax whilst any increase in value in the company's shares (enhanced by permitted retentions of income) must eventually suffer capital gains tax.

It follows that on the death of a controlling director a considerable sum of money may have to be found to pay estate duty for which it has not been possible to make adequate provision.

Under Section 161 of Income Tax Act, 1952, the cost to a company of providing any benefit for a director has to be treated as part of the director's income for tax purposes, but an exception is the cost of the provision for the director or for his spouse, children and dependants of any pension on death or retirement. Under Section 379 or 388 the provision of retirement benefits are effectively excluded, but the definition of 'retirement benefits' (Section 390) does not include benefit payable solely by reason of the death or disability of the director while in the service of the company.

It follows that it is possible for a company to provide death in service benefits for the family of a controlling director with the tax and estate duty advantages associated with the 'Top-Hat' arrangement described in Chapters 16 and 17. If properly arranged, premiums can be paid from the retained profits of the company without charging the director the additional liability and with no estate duty being payable on the policy proceeds.

The policy used would normally be a whole life assurance and would be taken out by the company as trustee on the life of the controlling director. The benefits would be split into two parts, (a) if the death of the director occurs in service, (b) if his death occurred out of service.

The reason for splitting the benefit into two parts is to satisfy the requirements that the benefit is only payable on death *in service*.

When the director has retired from service, cover would operate under the second part for the benefit *of the company*, as in the case of 'key man insurance' illustrated above, the proceeds on death being taxable in the company's hands.

12

Buying a House

BUYING A house usually calls for a sum running into several thousands of pounds, which is, in most cases, beyond the potential owner's capital resources. Even when he has sufficient money, it may be inconvenient or unprofitable to release it by selling investments. Usually, therefore, a loan has to be raised, either from a bank, or by means of a mortgage from a local council, building society or insurance company. Bank loans are normally repayable over relatively short periods, normally not exceeding five to seven years, and are not, therefore, a suitable source of finance for house purchase for the majority of people. On the whole, building societies and insurance companies offer the best facilities for house purchase.

Building Society Mortgage

The normal advance is 75 per cent on reasonably modern or new houses valued at up to say, £7,000; on older property a lower percentage is usually offered. The advance may be increased, up to, say, 90 or 95 per cent, where an acceptable guarantee can be given, such as insurance companies provide in the form of an indemnity policy (described below).

The usual method of redeeming a building society mortgage is by level annual or monthly payments which cover interest and repayment of capital. Because the payments are equalized in amount, the portion representing interest is very high in the early years and reduces in bigger steps as the repayment of capital progresses. This means that tax relief, which is calculated on the interest content of each payment, is on a reducing scale as well. The rate of interest charged can usually be varied subject to, say, three months' notice, which benefits the borrower when interest rates are falling but means increased payments or an extension of the payment period when they rise. Additional sums can be paid at any time to speed up repayment or reduce future payments, depending on the rules of the various societies.

The main advantage of the building society mortgage is its flexibility in accommodating lump sums to speed up the process of repayment. The variable rate of interest is also beneficial if market rates are high at the time the mortgage is effected and likely to ease later. Possible disadvantages are the annual reductions in the amount of each payment which can be set off against tax, and the fact that, allowing for sufficient life assurance to cover the capital outstanding from time to time, it normally costs more over the total period than the insurance company mortgage explained below, if the borrower is paying sufficient tax at the standard rate. Building societies do not insist upon life assurance cover being provided by the borrower, but no responsible person would neglect to ensure that the debt on his house was fully discharged in the event of death. Policies specially designed to cover building society mortgages have been illustrated in Chapter 9.

If the mortgage protection policy is effected by payment of a single premium, most building societies will agree to increase the loan by the amount of this and adjust the schedule of repayments over the mortgage period accordingly. The policy is then assigned to the building society.

BUILDING SOCIETY MONTHLY REPAYMENT FOR EACH £100 BORROWED

Repayment term (years)	*Interest rate* 6%	6½%	7%
15	17/2	17/9	18/4
20	14/7	15/2	15/9
25	13/1	13/8	14/4
30	12/2	12/10	13/6

Insurance Company Mortgage

The granting of such loans is part of an insurance company's investment policy, but the extent to which companies are willing to do business on this basis will be influenced by the investment conditions of the day. One important consideration from their point of view is the current facilities for long-term investment at, say, 6 per cent or 6½ per cent interest. Although mortgages are usually effected for terms up to 20 or 25 years, a large number are probably repaid through change of house ownership long before the original period expires, when conditions for re-investing capital may be less favourable.

Not all insurance companies lend on mortgages, but those which do tend to be more generous than building societies in the percentages they offer. In this type of mortgage the capital remains outstanding for the whole of the mortgage period and interest is charged accordingly. The mortgage is redeemed on the maturity of an endowment assurance policy which can be effected, either with or without profits, for a basic sum assured equal to the amount advanced. The policy is, of course, assigned to the insurance company.

At first sight, this may seem to be an expensive method of repayment, but it must be remembered that the endowment premium represents capital repayments discounted at interest. Thus the interest allowed in the insurance premiums cancels out part of the interest charged on the loan. On this basis, two sets of tax relief are being obtained: one on the loan interest which, allowing for loss of earned income relief at two-ninths, works out (if tax is paid at 8*s* 3*d* in the £), at 6*s* 5*d* on each £1 of interest, and the other on the endowment premiums which, on the same reckoning, works out at about 3*s* 4*d* on each £1 of premium. This last tax allowance has the effect of narrowing the gap between the net interest debited to the borrower and the net interest credited to him in the policy and, therefore, the effective cost of borrowing. If the loan is being repaid by a with-profits policy, it is possible that the borrower will at the end of the day put back into his pocket more than he has taken out. But although a with-profits policy will almost certainly pay off in the long run, when it comes to buying a house the insurance company will, unfortunately, insist upon the amount it advances being fully covered by the basic sum assured, so that over the mortgage period the actual repayments are greater. At a time when money is likely to be very short this can be a serious obstacle, but even if a non-profit policy is all that the borrower can afford to begin with, he should change it to with-profits as soon as he is able to meet the extra cost. Some insurance companies are willing to give larger loans, or to extend the repayment period at outset, against the greater security that a with-profits policy affords them and this may make it easier for the borrower to settle for a with-profits policy at outset.

At one time, this type of mortgage was available only from insurance companies, but a number of building societies are now also willing to lend, in certain circumstances, on the collateral security of an endowment policy assigned to them. No doubt this is because they recognize that the endowment method of repayment is advantageous for certain people, although it cannot be so for the building societies themselves if it reduces the immediate flow of capital repayments. Turnover in house ownership, however, is such that the average period of individual loans is only about eight years.

If the borrower is under about 45 years of age the endowment method of repayment (assuming sufficient standard rate income tax is payable) is cheaper than the normal method of repayment to a building society and offers the advantage that life assurance protection is automatically included. If the policy participates in profits, there is a cash sum to come on repayment of the loan and this can provide a useful fund for major repairs or improvements.

Recently it has become possible to use as collateral security for house mortgages a whole life, instead of an endowment, policy. Under these circumstances, the loan may never have to be repaid, but the policy must be for such an amount that, at the end of the normal repayment period, it has acquired a surrender value equal to the loan. This means that the annual premiums will be higher than those required to provide an equivalent sum on the maturity of an endowment policy. On the other hand, the borrower gains two advantages. First, his life assurance cover is higher per £1 of premium than under an endowment assurance, and secondly, he is able to maintain this cover in full at the end of the normal mortgage period if the policy is not surrendered.

Indemnity Policy

If a building society is willing to advance, say, 80 per cent of valuation and the applicant requires 90 per cent, the building society may be prepared to lend the balance against the additional security of an indemnity policy issued to the building society by an insurance company. The policy indemnifies the building society against any loss it may suffer in respect of *the additional advance*, so protecting the society against the risk of a forced sale at a price which does not enable it to recover the full sum lent. The premium would normally be between 4½ per cent and 5½ per cent of the sum at risk, depending on the term of the mortgage, and this would, of course, be charged to the borrower.

Completion Guarantee

Many contracts for the sale of houses are not completed on the due date, and there can be various reasons for this. It may be that the buyer cannot complete his mortgage arrangements on time, or perhaps the sale of his own house has been delayed. In some cases, this delay may cause considerable inconvenience. To cover this risk it is possible to obtain from a company specially set up for the purpose a guarantee that the seller receives the purchase price on the precise date when it is due. If the buyer fails to complete his contract on time, the guarantee becomes effective. This guarantee is available to sellers of moderately priced houses at a current cost of 12*s* 6*d* for each £100 on the amount guaranteed up to £5,000, and 10*s* per cent on the amount over this figure. Thus, on a house costing £5,000, the premium would be £31 5*s* 0*d* and on a house costing £8,000 it would be £46 5*s* 0*d*.

The following six plans illustrate the methods of repayment discussed above.

PLAN IX

This illustrates the cost of repayment on the building society method, without life assurance cover. For comparative purposes, it is assumed that tax relief is at 8s 3d in the £, as in the other examples, although in general the method is more suitable for someone paying tax at a lower rate.

LOAN OF £5,000 OVER 20 YEARS AT 6½ PER CENT BY CAPITAL REPAYMENT

Annual repayment £455

Overall Cost	£9,100	0s	0d
Less loan of £5,000	5,000	0	0
	4,100	0	0
Less: tax relief on interest content	1,691	5	0
	2,408	15	0
Add: back loss of two-ninths earned income allowance	375	16	8
Net cost of borrowing	£2,784	11s	8d

PLAN X

This illustrates the cost of the non-profit endowment method of repayment for comparison with Plan IX. In this and the following example it is assumed that the borrower is aged 35 next birthday.

Loan of £5,000 Over 20 Years at 6½ per cent in Conjunction with £5,000 Without-profit Endowment Assurance

	£	s	d
Interest on £5,000 at 6½ per cent	£325	0s	0d
Less: tax deducted	134	1	3
Net interest payable	190	18	9
Annual premium	192	10	0
	383	8	9
Less: tax saving on premium	31	15	3
	351	13	6
Add: back loss of two-ninths earned income allowance	29	15	10
Total net cost per annum	£381	9s	4d

	£	s	d
Total net cost over 20 years	£7,629	6s	8d
Less: original loan of £5,000 repaid on maturity of policy	5,000	0	0
Ultimate net cost	£2,629	6s	8d

PLAN XI

It is assumed in this case that by taking out a with-profits policy, the borrower is able to obtain an extended repayment term of 25 years. Because of this, the additional net cost per annum is relatively small compared with Plan X, whilst a substantial sum by way of bonuses is released on redemption.

LOAN OF £5,000 OVER 25 YEARS AT 6½ PER CENT IN CONJUNCTION WITH £5,000 WITH-PROFIT ENDOWMENT ASSURANCE

Interest on £5,000 at 6½ per cent	£325	0s	0d			
Less: tax deducted	134	1	3			
Net interest payable	190	18	9			
Annual premium	220	0	0			
	410	18	9			
Less: tax saving on premium	36	6	0			
	374	12	9			
Add: back loss of two-ninths earned income allowance	29	15	10			
Total net cost per annum	£404	8s	7d			
Total net cost over 25 years				£10,110	14s	7d
Less: original loan of £5,000 repaid on maturity of policy				5,000	0	0
Final net cost				5,110	14	7
Deduct: estimated bonuses at maturity				4,375	0	0
Estimated ultimate net cost				£735	14s	7d

PLAN XII

Although this calls for the highest annual outlay, it is the most economical method of repayment in the end, as will be seen by comparing in the illustration below the total outgoings with the estimated cash returned in bonuses at maturity.

LOAN OF £5,000 OVER 20 YEARS AT 6½ PER CENT IN CONJUNCTION WITH £5,000 WITH-PROFIT ENDOWMENT ASSURANCE

Interest on £5,000 at 6½ per cent	£325	0s	0d			
Less: tax deducted	134	1	3			
Net interest payable	190	18	9			
Annual premium	265	0	0			
	455	18	9			
Less: tax saving on premium	43	14	6			
	412	4	3			
Add: back loss of two-ninths earned income allowance	29	15	10			
Total net cost per annum	£442	0s	1d			
Total net cost over 20 years				£8,840	1s	8d
Less: original loan of £5,000 repaid on maturity of policy				5,000	0	0
Final net cost				3,840	1	8
Deduct: estimated bonuses at maturity				3,500	0	0
Estimated ultimate net cost				£340	1s	8d

PLAN XIII

In this case, a whole life assurance instead of an endowment is used as collateral security for the mortgage. Although the annual repayments are higher, the plan provides more cover per £1 of premium than those based on repayment by endowment assurance and this cover can be maintained in full at the end of the normal mortgage period. The loan, therefore, may never have to be repaid during the borrower's lifetime, but the policy must be for such an amount that at the end of the normal repayment period it has acquired a surrender value equal to the loan.

LOAN OF £20,000 OVER 25 YEARS AT 6½ PER CENT IN CONJUNCTION WITH WHOLE LIFE ASSURANCE WITHOUT PROFITS

Interest on £20,000 at 6½ per cent	£1,300 0s 0d	
Less: tax deducted	536 5 0	
Net interest payable	763 15 0	
(Sum assured £51,500)		
Annual premium	851 10 0	
	1,615 5 0	
Less: tax saving on premiums	140 10 0	
	1,474 15 0	
Add: back loss of two-ninths earned income allowance	119 3 0	
Total net cost per annum	£1,593 18s 0d	
Total net cost over 25 years		£39,847 10s 0d
Less: surrender value of policy		20,033 0 0
Total net cost if policy surrendered		£19,814 10s 0d

PLAN XIV

This is on the same basis as the preceding plan, but the whole life assurance is taken out with profits and one half of the company's current rate of bonus is allowed towards making up the surrender value. The initial sum assured required to support the loan is thus correspondingly reduced.

Loan of £20,000 Over 25 Years at 6½ per cent in Conjunction with Whole Life Assurance With Profits

Interest on £20,000 at 6½ per cent	£1,300 0s 0d	
Less: tax deducted	536 5 0	
Net interest payable	763 15 0	
(Sum assured £29,400 with profits)		
Annual premium	853 17 0	
	1,617 12 0	
Less: tax saving on premiums	140 18 0	
	1,476 14 0	
Add: back loss of two-ninths earned income allowance	199 3 0	
Total net cost per annum	£1,595 17s 0d	
Total net cost over 25 years		£39,896 5s 0d
Less: surrender value of basic policy		11,930 0 0
surrender value of one half of bonuses		8,070 0 0
		20,000 0 0
Deduct: surrender value of other half of bonuses payable in cash		8,070 0 0
Estimated ultimate net cost if policy surrendered		£11,826 5s 0d

13

Paying for School Fees

THE PLANS included in this chapter illustrate various ways in which the cost of a child's education can be planned ahead by payments out of current income. The first two examples show what can be done by the parent wholly out of his own income; the third example shows the advantages secured in certain circumstances where a relation or friend can be persuaded to enter into a deed of covenant.

The principle adopted is to spread the cost of the fees over as long a period as possible, starting well before the time that schooling begins and finishing just before it ends. For this purpose, an endowment assurance policy is taken out which participates in profits. When the school fees are due, the money for them will be advanced by the insurance company term by term against the security of the policy. This money is paid to the insured and not direct to the school, so that it remains fully under the parent's control. An essential requirement of any plan of this sort is that it should be completely flexible, so that it can be varied, added to or discontinued according to circumstances, which so often change. For this reason, the normal 'educational policy' illustrated by companies in their prospectuses is not altogether suitable. It is merely a short-term endowment policy maturing before the time school begins and providing for payment of the sum assured in instalments over the fee-paying period, instead of as a lump sum. If a series of such policies were taken out to mature in the first, second, third, fourth and fifth year of school a better spread of cost would be achieved, but the policies would not lend themselves easily to adjustment and the full value of profit sharing (as well as the premium rate reduction on a single larger policy) would be lost. In the plans suggested here, full use is made of borrowing facilities so that the policy is kept in force to accumulate bonuses for as long as possible. This achieves maximum spread of cost and maximum saving of income tax.

Two further points should be considered when using a with-profits policy in this way. First, the sum payable in the event of death will start on the low side and build up year by year with bonuses. It is sensible, therefore, to include additional protection in the form of an income benefit as illustrated in Chapter 9. Secondly, the full success of the plan depends on bonuses which are not guaranteed. It is wise, then, not to assume that present bonus rates will continue without abatement but to see that the plan incorporates a safety margin against adverse experience. Furthermore, when school time comes, the fees themselves may turn out to be much higher than presently estimated, in which case surplus will be needed.

PLAN XV

A parent, aged 30 next birthday, wants to provide for his newborn child public school fees of £500 per annum for five years, starting in 13 years' time.

The parent takes out a with-profits endowment assurance policy for a basic sum assured of £1,650, payable at the end of 17 years or previous death. The total estimated sum at maturity is £2,631, which covers the total fees payable and leaves a margin of safety. The policy incorporates additional life assurance protection in the form of income benefit of £100 per annum, which is tax free and payable for the remainder of the term. In years 13 to 17 inclusive, a total of £2,500 is borrowed against the surrender value of the policy and it is assumed for purposes of the illustration that the gross interest charged by the insurance company is 6½ per cent.

Endowment Assurance With Profits to Provide Public School Fees
Male, aged 30 next birthday

BENEFITS:

Sum guaranteed at end of 17 years or previous death	£1,650 0s 0d
Estimated bonus additions assuming an average rate of bonus of 70s per cent per annum simple	981 15 0
	£2,631 15s 0d

COST:

Yearly premium (monthly premium £8 18s 4d)	£104 7s 4d
Income tax saving	17 4 4
Net sum invested yearly	87 3 0
Total net outlay over 17 years	£1,481 11s 0d
Estimated profit on investment Including £3,350/1,650 life assurance	£1,150 4s 0d

Life Assurance Cover

The benefits payable on death before the plan is completed would be:

(*a*) £1,650

(*b*) Bonuses to date on £1,650.

(*c*) £100 per annum maintenance income (tax free) payable for remainder of term of policy.

Thus, the total benefits payable at the commencement of the policy would be £3,350.

SCHEDULE SHOWING HOW THE PLAN WORKS

Age of child	*Fees required*	*Gross premium*	*Net premium*	*Net interest*	*Net annual cost*
	£	£ s d	£ s d	£ s d	£ s d
0		104 7 4	87 3 0		87 3 0
1		,,	,,		,,
2		,,	,,		,,
3		,,	,,		,,

Age of child	*Fees required*	*Gross premium*	*Net premium*	*Net interest*	*Net annual cost*
	£	£ s d	£ s d	£ s d	£ s d
4		104 7 4	87 3 0		87 3 0
5		”	”		”
6		”	”		”
7		”	”		”
8		”	”		”
9		”	”		”
10		”	”		”
11		”	”		”
12		”	”		”
13	500	”	”		”
14	500	”	”	19 2 0	106 5 0
15	500	”	”	38 4 0	125 7 0
16	500	”	”	57 6 0	144 9 0
17	500	–	–	76 7 0	76 7 0
	2,500	1,774 4 8	1,481 11 0	190 19 0	1,672 10 0

Summary of Plan XV

Receipts

Total Fees provided	£2,500 0*s* 0*d*
Expected surplus on maturity of policy	131 15 0
Total sums received	£2,631 15*s* 0*d*

Expenditure

The net annual cost at the beginning of the plan is £87 3*s* 0*d*, rising after the school time begins to a maximum of £144 9*s* 0*d*

Total net cost is therefore	£1,672 10*s* 0*d*
This shows a saving of	£959 5*s* 0*d*

In addition the plan has provided full protection in the event of death.

PLAN XVI

The parent in Plan XV wants to provide, in addition to the above, preparatory boarding school fees of £350 per annum payable from years 8 to 12.

ENDOWMENT ASSURANCE WITH PROFITS TO PROVIDE PREPARATORY BOARDING AND PUBLIC SCHOOL FEES

Male, aged 30 next birthday

BENEFITS:

Sum guaranteed at the end of 17 years or previous death	£2,800 0s 0d
Estimated bonus additions (assuming an average rate of bonus of 70s per cent per annum simple)	1,666 0 0
	£4,466 0s 0d

COST:

Yearly premium (monthly premium £14 19s 2d)	£175 1s 9d
Income tax saving	28 17 9
Net sum invested yearly	146 4 0
Total net outlay over 17 years	£2,485 8s 0d
Estimated profit on investment	
Including £5,350/2,800 life assurance	£1,980 12s 0d

Life Assurance Cover

The benefits payable on death before the plan is completed would be:

(*a*) £2,800.
(*b*) Bonuses to date on £2,800.
(*c*) £150 per annum maintenance income (tax free) payable for remainder of term of policy.

Thus, the total benefits payable at the commencement of the policy would be £5,350.

Schedule Showing how the Plan Works

Age of child	*Fees required*	*Gross premium*	*Net premium*	*Net interest*	*Net annual cost*
	£	£ s d	£ s d	£ s d	£ s d
0		175 1 9	146 4 0		146 4 0
1		”	”		”
2		”	”		”
3		”	”		”
4		”	”		”
5		”	”		”
6		”	”		”
7		”	”		”
8	350	”	”		”
9	350	”	”	13 7 0	159 11 0
10	350	”	”	26 15 0	172 19 0
11	350	”	”	40 2 0	186 6 0
12	350	”	”	53 9 0	199 13 0
13	500	”	”	66 17 0	213 1 0
14	500	”	”	85 18 0	232 2 0
15	500	”	”	105 0 0	251 4 0
16	500	”	”	124 2 0	270 6 0
17	500	–	–	143 4 0	143 4 0
	4,250	2,976 9 9	2,485 8 0	658 14 0	3,144 2 0

Summary of Plan XVI

Receipts

Total Fees provided	£4,250 0*s* 0*d*
Expected surplus on maturity of policy	216 0 0
Total sums received	£4,466 0*s* 0*d*

Expenditure

The net annual cost at the beginning of the plan is £146 4*s* 0*d*, rising after the school time begins to a maximum of £270 6*s* 0*d*

Total net cost is therefore	£3,144 2*s* 0*d*
This shows a saving of	£1,321 18*s* 0*d*

In addition the plan has provided full protection in the event of death.

Immediate Loans

The plans illustrated assume that early action can be taken before schooling starts. What if no such provision has been made? Fortunately it is possible in these circumstances to get an immediate loan or the guarantee of one a short time ahead.

When fees are required immediately one of the best schemes provides an unsecured loan to pay school fees up to an agreed amount over a five-year term. The minimum loan is normally £1,000 and the maximum is restricted to one year's salary. The fees are paid direct to the school and the parent takes out an endowment policy equal to the amount of loan required to pay these fees, the proceeds of which would be sufficient to repay the loan at the end of 10 years or the parent's earlier death.

Another type of scheme is available to holders of trust units and investment trust shares, who can borrow from the insurance company up to one year's income against the securities held, repaying by means of an endowment policy (with- or without-profits) over a maximum period of 25 years.

The advantage of the latter scheme to those who can take advantage of it is the extended term of repayment and the lower interest rate normally charged in comparison with the other schemes through which unsecured loans are given.

Trustee Scheme

This scheme makes it possible to use capital discounted at a gross rate of interest in meeting the cost of future education. The scheme is operated by a consultancy organization specializing in education finance.

Although it may not be practicable to nominate a particular school, most parents have a rough idea of the amount of fees which they expect to have to pay for the type of school to which they are planning to send their child. Fees at the majority of independent public schools are at present in the region of £600 a year. The illustration shows the cost of paying for fees of £600 for five years from the age of 13 at different periods in advance. The capital required is paid to the trustees of the scheme who invest the money in an annuity policy with an insurance company to guarantee the required fees at the right time. The settlor has no interest in the annuity policy except in so far as is necessary for the terms of the trust deed to be complied with. A bank executor and trustee company acts as trustees of the scheme until the annuity policy is assigned for the payment of school fees.

Capital payments under the scheme can be made not only by the parent but by anybody, e.g. a friend, a grandparent or even the parent's employer. (In the latter case, however, unless in the form of a loan, there is a taxable benefit to the employee.)

The scheme is available for all schools to which payment of fees may be made in sterling currency without exchange control permission.

PLAN XVII

This shows how the cost of future education can be cut by paying a capital sum under trusteeship arrangements not identified with a particular school. The plan is therefore suitable for the parent who, for one reason or another, wishes to postpone a definite decision on choice of school or who wishes to send his child to a school which does not itself offer similar facilities.

Assuming fees of £600 a year for five years the cost of school fees if paid on a termly basis would come to £3,000.

If paid under trustee scheme the cost at current rates would be:

	Cost	*Saving*
(*a*) Thirteen years before entry	£1,577 3*s* 1*d*	£1,422 16*s* 11*d*
(*b*) Ten years before entry	£1,822 19*s* 5*d*	£1,177 0*s* 7*d*
(*c*) Five years before entry	£2,288 2*s* 9*d*	£ 711 17*s* 3*d*
(*d*) On entry to the school	£2,795 8*s* 5*d*	£204 11*s* 7*d*

Payment may be made for any amount of fees and for any number of terms. Payment may also be made for University fees.

Notes:

(1) The trustees do not need to know where the child is going to school until one month before the first term's fees are due to be paid. When the school has been nominated the fees are paid direct to the school.

If the actual fees are greater than the amount provided under the scheme, the parent pays the difference direct to the school.

If the fees are lower than the amount provided, the difference between the amount originally paid and the amount which would have been needed at that time to provide the actual fees will be refunded.

The scheme cannot be extended to provide 'extras' or other expenses. These are paid by the parent when they arise.

(2) If the child should die, the full amount paid is immediately refunded. If the parent wishes to withdraw from the scheme for any other reason before the child is due to go to school, not less than 95 per cent of the original payment less the small administrative costs will be refunded.

If the parent wishes to withdraw when the child is actually due to go to school, e.g., due to obtaining a free place at a grammar school, at least the original capital sum will be refunded. If the child goes to school for a shorter time than planned, the difference between the amount originally paid and the amount which would have been required for the fees actually provided will be refunded.

(3) The Trust Deed provides that if the fees at the school to which the child goes are lower than those provided by the Deed, the settlor will be refunded the difference between the amount which he paid and the amount which would have been needed to provide the actual fees required.

It follows, therefore, that if no fees are payable then the settlor will be refunded the full amount which he paid.

This is the minimum guaranteed repayment. If it should become impossible, due to legislation, to use the money for its original purpose, it may be possible to break the terms of the Trust and for the settlor to receive, in addition to the capital sum, the interest earned to date.

(4) The dates of payment can be altered to provide a smaller amount by an earlier date or a larger amount by a later date. These amounts will be calculated according to the original payment and no financial loss will be incurred beyond a small fee which is charged for re-writing the terms of the policy.

(5) If the child is moved from one school to another the payment of fees can be transferred (a small transfer fee may be charged). Benefits can be transferred from one child to another at the request of the settlor if he elects option (*a*) with regard to retaining his right to surrender the

policy as explained under 'Income Tax and Estate Duty' below. If he elects option (*b*) an irrevocable trust is created for the education of the child concerned as long as he or she is alive and able to receive the benefit of it. Therefore, under option (*b*) the benefits can normally only be transferred in the event of the death of the child originally named.

Income Tax and Estate Duty

Neither the income tax liability of the parent nor the child is affected in any way at all. The payments are considered as the income of the school to which the child goes. The Trust Deed, however, contains a 'saving clause' stating that if the present law is changed, whereby charitable institutions are exempt from tax on their income, the settlor may be required to pay the difference between the amount shown on the schedule to the Trust Deed and the actual amount received under the annuity policy if the latter should be lower.

Estate duty will be payable on the capital sum while the parent or settlor retains the option to recover his payment at will.

The parent or settlor will, therefore, be offered the following options:

(*a*) To retain his right to ask for the surrender of the payment at any time before the child goes to school and thereby retain the capital within his estate.

or (*b*) To forego his right to ask for the surrender of the payment and thereby segregate the capital from his estate.

In either case the settlor retains his right to recover his full payment immediately in the event of the death of the child and to receive the surrender value at the time of going to school if a non-fee paying school should be chosen.

14

Short- to Medium-term Saving

PLAN XVIII

A man aged 40 has made sufficient provision for his family in the event of death and can afford to start saving. His intention is to do so for the next 15 years and he is prepared to leave the money he saves untouched until the end of that period. He therefore seeks an investment likely to produce the best result in the time allowed, with complete security of capital.

Endowment assurance with profits should be the first choice in these conditions. If the saver pays tax at the standard rate, the relief allowed at present more than pays for the cost of life assurance allowed in the premiums. At the rate of bonus assumed (which is below the level of some of the most recent declarations) the policy shows an exceptionally good return, as will be seen from the example. These bonuses are not guaranteed, but with most of the leading companies they are supported by substantial reserves which minimize the risk of early disappointment. This is of special importance when considering a suitable investment during a period of economic uncertainty, when it may be some time before a definite trend is established in ordinary shares which would produce comparable results. The key features which commend this plan are, therefore, security of capital and a high predictable rate of growth over the period chosen.

Policy Description: Chapter 6

15 Year Endowment Assurance With Profits

Male aged 41 next birthday

BENEFITS:

Sum assured payable at the end of 15 years or on previous death	£1,408 0*s* 0*d*
Estimated bonus additions, assuming an average rate of bonus of 70*s* per cent per annum simple	739 4 0
Total estimated sum at maturity	£2,147 4*s* 0*d*

INVESTMENT:

Yearly premium (monthly premium £8 10*s* 10*d*)	£100 0*s* 0*d*
Income tax saving (allowing for 7 per cent limitation)	16 5 0
Net sum invested yearly	£83 15*s* 0*d*
Total net sum invested over 15 years	£1,256 5*s* 0*d*

Estimated profit on investment

Including life assurance of £1,408	£890 19*s* 0*d*

(Increased each year by bonus additions)

Estimated Yield on Investment

The estimated return from this policy is equivalent to an investment yielding almost 6½ per cent per annum net of income tax. If this figure is grossed-up at the standard rate of tax (8*s* 3*d* in the £) the yield is 11 per cent per annum.

PLAN XIX

A man aged 40 wishes to save the same amount as in Plan XVIII, but to continue his saving until he reaches retirement age in 25 years' time and also to make provision for his family should he die before the plan is completed.

Where the savings period is 25 years, the advantage of endowment assurance over, say, a unit trust is much less certain; consequently, the need for substantial life assurance cover may be a decisive factor in choosing this method of saving. The endowment policy gets off to a flying start with the probability of immediate high bonuses but, by the end of the day, the unit trust will have had plenty of time to catch up. Moreover, when considering so long a period, the saver will be less sure of his ability or desire to maintain premiums throughout, on which the full value of his endowment policy depends. For this reason, it is a wise precaution to choose a policy which provides on discontinuance for the paid-up sum assured to continue to participate in profits. This plan, like the preceding one, is quite unsuitable for early cash withdrawal.

Policy Description: Chapter 6

25 YEAR ENDOWMENT ASSURANCE WITH PROFITS

Male aged 41 next birthday

BENEFITS:

Sum assured payable at the end of 25 years or on previous death	£2,222	0*s*	0*d*
Estimated bonus additions, assuming an average rate of bonus of 60*s* per cent per annum compound	2,338	0	0
Total estimated sum at maturity	£4,560	0*s*	0*d*

INVESTMENT:

Yearly premium (monthly premium £8 10*s* 10*d*)	£100	0*s*	0*d*
Income tax saving	16	10	0
Net sum invested yearly	£83	10*s*	0*d*
Total net sum invested over 25 years	£2,087	10*s*	0*d*

Estimated Profit on Investment

Including life assurance of £2,222	£2,472	10*s*	0*d*

(Increased each year by bonus additions)

Estimated Yield on Investment

The estimated return from this policy is equivalent to an investment yielding over 5½ per cent per annum net of income tax. If this figure is grossed-up at the standard rate of tax (8*s* 3*d* in the £) the yield is almost 9½ per cent per annum.

15

Medium- to Long-term Saving

THE PLANS illustrated in this chapter are a selection of those combining the advantages of life assurance with investment linked to the value of ordinary shares. They are essentially designed for the long-term rather than short-term investor and this particularly applies to Plan XXII.

The criticism most frequently levelled against an ordinary endowment policy as a method of saving is that the money paid out when the policy matures does not sufficiently compensate the saver for the fall in the value of the total sum he has invested over the savings period. This criticism usually overlooks the fact that the total sum invested has been spread over the whole of the period of inflation, so that the average difference between the value of the currency paid in and the value of the currency taken out is much less than appears at first sight. It also usually overlooks the fact that a substantial portion of the premiums has been paid by the Inland Revenue, and that the saver has been covered for a substantial sum in the event of death. But it is true that, since World War II, the fall in the value of money has been so steep and persistent that investment in ordinary shares would normally have produced much better results.

There are, basically, two reasons for this. First, when the value of money falls the value of almost any commodity bought with money, including shares in those commodities, rises, and secondly, because inflation generally brings increased industrial profits, which means larger dividends. Industrial shares therefore provide in this sense an automatic hedge against inflation.

The policies illustrated in the previous chapter also provide a hedge against inflation but, depending on the degree of inflation experienced, the hedge is less automatic. This is because all the risks are taken from the saver and borne by the life fund as a whole which, year by year, must carry forward sufficient reserves to cover its immediate, as well as future, commitments. And also because both new and old policyholders share on a roughly equal footing in the surplus available for distribution as profit.

The pattern of the past is unlikely to be repeated on anything like the same scale again. At a time of economic uncertainty, when progress in ordinary shares has been temporarily halted, the conventional with-profits policy is at an advantage because it has reserves to draw upon to maintain future bonuses. But so long as spectacular results are not expected, the equity-linked contract offers a sound basis for long-term saving.

The link with ordinary shares is achieved by identifying the savings element in the contracts with the fortunes of a specified unit trust. In considering the type of contract it is, therefore, important in the first instance to understand precisely what a unit trust is, how it is controlled and how management costs are met.

The description which follows is taken from the *Directory of Unit Trusts*, by kind permission of the Association of Unit Trust Managers.

What a Unit Trust is

'A unit trust is a convenient and economical method of investment by which money subscribed by many people is pooled in a fund, the investment and management of which are subject to the strict legal provisions of a trust deed. The fund is invested in securities on behalf of the subscribers by a management company. The investments so acquired are held by a trustee, which is generally a well-known bank or insurance company. The management company and the trustee, who must be effectively independent of each other, are parties to the trust deed which sets out their respective responsibilities towards the subscribers to the trust fund, and details the rules for the operation of the trust.

'Before its units may be offered for sale to the public, a unit trust must be authorized by the Board of Trade. This power of control is given to the Board by an Act of Parliament and is exercised by means of requirements made from time to time by the officials of the Board. The Board of Trade will not issue a certificate of authorization unless it is satisfied that the trust deed by which the trust is constituted is drawn in accordance with its requirements.

'The Act, implemented by the Board's requirements, stipulates that the trust deed shall provide *inter alia*: for the provision of funds for future management expenses; for the audit and circulation to unit holders of the accounts of the managers in relation to the trust; for the manner in which the sale and the repurchase prices of units and the advertised yield is calculated; for the examination by the trustee of all advertisements; and for changes in management if the trustee certifies that it is in the interest of the subscribers to the trust that this should happen.

'Unit trusts vary as to detail but the general principles behind all of them are as follows:

'Through his subscription to the trust fund, each subscriber acquires a fractional interest in the block of securities in which the fund is invested, while the dividends received from the investments form the income of the trust. The net income is paid to all investors in the trust fund in proportion to the size of their holdings. The primary functions of the trustee are to ensure that the terms of the trust deed are observed, to act as custodian of the capital and income of the trust, to hold in its name the securities in which money subscribed by the public to the trust fund has been invested by the managers, and to take responsibility for the register of unit holders. The manager is responsible financially and otherwise for the administration of the unit trust, for calculating the unit offered and bid price, for preparing income distributions, for managing the investment portfolio of the trust fund, and for maintaining a market in the units of the trust, including the responsibility for repurchasing any units which holders wish to realize.

'The services which the trustee and the managers perform for the unit holder have of course to be paid for, but the charges which may be made are strictly controlled by the Board of Trade.

'These charges are taken by way of an initial service charge (which is included in the sale price of a unit), and a semi-annual management fee levied on the value of the fund and taken either out of income or capital. Over a 20-year life of a trust, the maximum which managers are currently permitted to charge by way of an initial service charge and management fees together is 13¼ per cent. Managers are also entitled to round off the price of a unit by 3*d* or 1 per cent (whichever is the lower) so that the quoted price may be expressed in a convenient fraction of a penny.

'From the charges permitted to be made, managers defray all the expenses of the administration of the unit trust (such as keeping a register of unit holders, distributing income half yearly and issuing unit certificates), of providing for investment management, of procuring subscriptions to the trust fund, of the trustee's fees and of paying commissions to accountants, banks, solicitors, stockbrokers and other recognized agents.

'Although the record of unit trusts has been outstandingly good over the last ten years, it should be realized that an investment in units neither guarantees an increasing income nor ensures continual capital appreciation. As the value of units is governed by the fluctuations in the price of the securities in which the trust fund is invested, the value of a holding of units when sold may be more or less than its original price.'

* * *

In Chapter 5, the various equity-linked contracts were roughly classified according to the guarantees they gave in terms of capital, interest and mortality. They should also be considered in relation to the capital gains tax.

In these contracts, as we have seen, units are earmarked for particular policyholders and the benefit of capital appreciation, but not necessarily dividends, accrues to the policyholder in the same way as if he had purchased the units direct. But the insurance company, not the policyholder, is the technical holder of the units and it follows that any capital gains realized on their subsequent disposal by the insurance company are taxable at the rate appropriate to the insurance company's life fund, which is limited to 37½ per cent. In some cases, however, the insurance company may not have to dispose of the units to pay out the policyholder.

If it has an expanding fund (and in the normal way life funds are continuously expanding) it should be able to retain units or equivalent securities as a long-term investment and pay the policyholder cash or purchase units for him out of its new premium income.

It would normally be in the insurance company's interest to deal with the matter in this way if the investment is a good one, because it could set off against the tax ultimately payable the net interest from dividends during the period of deferment. The effect is that, since the insurance company's potential tax liability is likely to be deferred far into the future, the rate at which it need make a deduction will probably be significantly lower than the actual rate provided by the Finance Act.

Insurance companies will, of course, reserve the right to deduct from the benefit due to the policyholder an amount equivalent to their tax liability, but it is reasonable to assume that where the insurance company can obtain relief in the way described the policyholder would benefit.

Plans XX and XXI illustrated below offer the possibility of a reduction in the normal rate of capital gains tax, but Plan XXII is quite different, as the purchase of units is dealt with separately by means of a loan from the insurance company redeemed on the maturity of a normal endowment assurance policy. In this case, therefore, the policyholder is the beneficial owner of the units and the tax position will be that applying to normal unit trust investment; i.e., tax is charged first on the trust on its switching operations and then on the unit holder when he sells, subject to his being able to claim double taxation relief.

The main difficulty in illustrating an equity-linked plan is to decide what rate of growth should be assumed. The post-war years have been an exceptional period for ordinary shares and it would be very unwise to take the average rate of appreciation over this period as a guide to the future. In the following examples it has been assumed, for immediate purposes of illustration, that the rate of accumulation, allowing for re-investment of dividends where appropriate, will be a little less than one-third what it has been over the last ten years. But this is not intended to be a forecast and is not, therefore, a valid basis for comparing value for money with the plans illustrated in the previous chapter, the results of which can be more accurately predicted.

PLAN XX

This is illustrated as an alternative to Plan XIX where there is a similar need for life assurance, but it is desired to link the savings element to a well-managed unit trust.

Under this plan, one-half of the premium is applied to secure units in a specified unit trust and the other half to whole life assurance. The whole of the premium is eligible for tax relief, just as if it were applied to a conventional endowment assurance.

The plan follows the principles ascribed to Type III explained in Chapter 6. Thus, after deducting the cost of the whole life assurance, 100 per cent of the balance is invested in units of the specified trust and the net dividends on these units are automatically re-invested as they fall due, so that the investor gets the benefit of any capital appreciation on these at the maturity of the policy. The *effect* of this part of the plan is, therefore, closely comparable to that achieved by direct investment of similar amounts in the same trust, except that the saver gets the benefit of life assurance tax relief and, it is thought, will not be liable for any capital gains tax when the plan is completed. Likewise, there is no insurance guarantee either as to capital or interest. The other part of the plan provides normal whole life assurance, but with the option to surrender this for a guaranteed cash sum at the end of the savings period.

Although the contract can be broken down in this way, it is expressed as a single entity and regarded by the company which issues it as a whole life assurance with an equity-linked with-profits element, to which 50 per cent of the total premium is allocated.

Policy Description: Chapter 6 (Equity-linked contracts: Type III)

EQUITY-LINKED WHOLE LIFE ASSURANCE

Male, aged 41 next birthday

CONTRIBUTIONS:

Monthly investment	£5 0s 0d
Income tax saving	16 6
Net sum invested monthly	£4 3s 6d
Total net contributions over 25 years	£1,252 10s 0d

APPLICATION OF CONTRIBUTIONS BY COMPANY

Each month, £2 10s 0d is applied as premiums to whole life assurance, with a guaranteed surrender value on completion of the plan; the balance of the contributions is fully applied to secure units in a specified unit trust.

BENEFITS:

(a) *On death before completion of plan*	
A guaranteed cash sum of	£1,383
plus	
the value of the units purchased	
(b) *On survival when the plan is completed*	
A guaranteed cash sum of	£589
plus	
the value of the units purchased. If, allowing for re-investment of dividends, they appreciate at 7½ per cent per annum the value of the units will be	£2,039
Total estimated cash sum	£2,628

The plan, however, is completely flexible, and the benefits can be dealt with in any of the following ways.

At maturity, the sum assured can be made paid-up for a reduced sum assured or fully maintained by payment of future contributions of £2 10s 0d a month; the units can be retained, or part-retained and part-surrendered for cash.

During the course of the plan, a portion of the units purchased can be encashed if, for example, funds are needed for house purchase, children's education, business needs or any emergency that may arise.

PLAN XXI

This is particularly suitable for the self-employed or professional man who wants to save a capital sum for retirement, as it includes permanent non-cancellable sickness and accident insurance at no additional premium cost. But the plan provides less valuable life assurance cover. For ease of comparison, the example is based on the same data as the two preceding plans.

Under this plan, a fixed proportion of the premiums is deemed to be invested in the units of a specified trust. The balance covers the cost of life assurance of a guaranteed minimum amount. The saver gets the benefit in cash of any appreciation in the value of the units at the time the plan is completed at maturity or earlier death, subject in both cases to the minimum guaranteed sum assured. Dividends are not automatically re-invested in securing further units for the benefit of the contributor, but are retained by the company, who pay bonuses from this dividend income. The plan includes the unusual feature that complete sickness and accident cover is provided out of the normal contribution qualifying for life assurance relief, the cost of this being met from the bonus fund. There are two advantages to the contributor in this system. One is that he gets, in effect, tax relief on the cost of sickness and accident insurance, for which tax relief is not normally available. The second is that sickness and accident insurance can be provided virtually at cost price, i.e., because a guaranteed premium is not charged it is not necessary for the insurance underwriter to allow a substantial margin for adverse experience. The margin the company requires is automatically provided in the 'with-profits pool' which can be drawn upon to the extent necessary to meet the actual claims which arise.

Policy Description: Chapter 6 (Equity-linked contracts: Type II)

EQUITY-LINKED ENDOWMENT ASSURANCE

Male, aged 40 next birthday

CONTRIBUTIONS:

Monthly investment	£5 0*s* 0*d*
Income tax saving	16 6
Net sum invested monthly	£4 3*s* 6*d*
Total net contributions over 25 years	£1,252 10*s* 0*d*

APPLICATION OF CONTRIBUTIONS BY COMPANY

Each month, £4 5*s* 0*d* of the amount contributed is deemed to be invested in units of a specified unit trust, so that the guaranteed amount allocated to the units over the period is £1,310.

BENEFITS:

(*a*) *On death before completion of plan*

either

a guaranteed cash sum of — £1,275, plus bonuses

or

the value of the units (including bonuses)

whichever is the greater

(*b*) *On survival when plan is completed*

either

a guaranteed cash sum — £1,275, plus bonuses

or

the value of the units (including bonuses)

whichever is the greater

If prices of the units increase at 5 per cent per annum, and bonuses amount to — £556

Total estimated cash sum is — £3,111

(*c*) *In the event of sickness or accident*

If the contributor is totally disabled by injury or sickness from carrying on his normal occupation, he will thereafter, so long as total disability continues, up to age 60, be entitled to benefits worth £4 19*s* 0*d* per week, i.e.,

(1) his contributions to the plan (approximately £1 3 0 per week) will be kept up for him free, and
(2) he will receive £3 16*s* 0*d* per week in cash.

Notes on Plan

General.—If contributions are discontinued after they have been paid for two full years, a paid-up policy is granted for the number of units allocated to the plan, plus any bonuses declared to date. Alternatively, the policy can be surrendered for its cash value, which takes into account the price of the units at the time.

Provision is made in the policy to deal with the position and adjust the benefits if, as a result of legislation or otherwise, investment in the units specified becomes impossible, or is made subject to capital gains tax.

All units purchased are an investment of the company and are not held upon trust for the contributor.

Sickness and Accident.—The sickness and accident insurance is an optional benefit included at no extra premium. If the option is selected, the bonuses payable will be reduced by reference to the sickness and accident claims of the contributors to the plan as a group (the insurance company estimates this would be about £150 in the example) but the allocation of units and their growth in value will not be affected by such claims.

Partial Disablement.—If the contributor is totally disabled from carrying out the duties pertaining to his normal occupation but chooses to do other work (at reduced earnings), he will receive proportional benefits.

A Different Approach to Equity-linked Investment

Just as it is possible to buy a house with the help of a loan from an insurance company and repay the loan by endowment assurance, as illustrated in Chapter 12, so the same procedure can be adopted in buying units in approved unit or investment trusts. This is illustrated in the plan below. At present, only one insurance company offers these facilities. The deposit required need not be in cash but may take the form of a transfer of units or shares of sufficient value approved by the insurance company. There are two schemes, one for units in a unit trust (as illustrated), and the other for acquiring units in an investment trust, the qualifications for which are more stringent.

PLAN XXII

This provides an opportunity for the investor who would like to acquire at once a block of units in a trust rather than a few at a time, but lacks the capital resources to do so. It is essentially (more so than Plans XX and XXI) a long-term investment, since the financial risk of short-term depreciation is magnified by the number of units purchased at a single price level. It is assumed that the borrower has a secure income of at least £2,000 a year, sufficient in shares or cash to put up the required deposit, and no intention of early withdrawal.

An endowment policy, which can be with or without profits, is taken out by the borrower for the amount of the loan. This policy, together with the investments, is charged to the insurance company under a mortgage deed. On maturity of the policy at the end of the loan period, or at earlier death, the proceeds are applied to redeem the loan and the investments are released. The policy is 25 years at the age of 40, as illustrated, reducing to ten years at the age of 55. This plan is not exempt from capital gains tax which will operate on the gain realized on the subsequent resale of the units.

Share Purchase With Mortgage

Male, aged 29 next birthday

A loan of £2,000 repayable over 25 years by an endowment assurance with profits for a sum assured of £2,000.

UNITS TO BE HELD BY THE COMPANY:

Provided from applicant's re-resources	£353 0s 0d	
Purchased with the advance	2,000 0 0	
Total amount invested in approved unit trust	£2,353 0s 0d	
Expenses, including stamp duty on the mortgage deed	£7 10s 0d	

OUTLAY:

Annual premium for with-profit endowment assurance	£86 13s 4d	
Income tax saving	14 6 0	£72 7s 4d
Interest at 6½ per cent on the advance	130 0 0	
Less: income tax	53 12 6	76 7 6
(assuming this is saved on 'unearned' income from the plan and other sources)		£148 14s 10d

BENEFITS:

For the purposes of illustrating this plan, it is assumed that capital will appreciate by 5 per cent per annum and income by 2½ per cent per annum.

INCOME:

Assuming a *present* gross yield on the units of 3 per cent net income from all units	£41 10*s* 0*d*
On the assumption made above, the net income will rise, in 25 years, to	£76 18*s* 0*d*
Thus, initially, the total net annual cost is	£107 4*s* 10*d*
This is estimated to reduce over the 25 years to	£71 16*s* 10*d*

CAPITAL:

Initial amount invested	£2,353 0*s* 0*d*
Capital appreciation at 5 per cent per annum	5,615 0 0
Estimated value of units in 25 years' time	7,968 0 0
Bonuses at maturity, assuming an average bonus rate of 58*s* per cent per annum simple	1,450 0 0
Total estimated capital in 25 years' time	£9,418 0*s* 0*d*

In the event of death during the currency of the plan, the loan would be repayed by the endowment sum assured. The units would then be released and transferred to the estate, together with bonuses declared on the policy up to the date of death.

16

Introduction

MANY OF the plans given in earlier chapters will provide a basis for retirement provision. Others will remain in force for the benefit of dependants and, in due course, release savings to them, though they may not have been originally designed for these purposes. Later in life, attention is naturally focused on the problems of providing for estate duty and securing an adequate retirement income. The plans illustrated in this section are designed with these specific objects in mind.

Estate Duty

The long-term solution to the problem of estate duty is provided by whole life assurance, which is equity-linked or with-profits, written under M.W.P.A. or similar trusts, under which the premiums qualify as 'normal expenditure' so that the proceeds are available in full to meet the estimated liability at the appropriate time. In other words an 'estate duty' fund is created. The same objective can be achieved if the policy is taken out on a 'life-of-another' basis, i.e. the wife takes out the policy on the life of her husband, the husband 'giving' her the premiums. Since no property passes on death there is no estate duty liability on the policy proceeds and the subject of the charge, if any, is the premiums given in the last seven years. This arrangement may be better if the premiums required for the estate duty fund are too large to qualify as 'normal expenditure' (clearly, it would be so if death occurred at an early stage).

Estate duty is a tax on property. It follows that the simplest way of avoiding this tax is to give away the property which attracts it. For example, if a person has assets of £50,000 and he gives away one-half of these to his wife and survives the gift by seven years, duty will only be charged on £25,000 on his death. If his wife feels she can afford to live on half that amount (perhaps with the help of an annuity) and, in turn, gives away in sufficiently good time the balance to her children, the total duty saved will be difference between duty on £50,000 and duty on separate estates of £25,000 and £12,500. Even if his wife keeps her money, a considerable saving will be made on the combined estates, because the duty on a single estate of £50,000 is £15,500, whereas on two separate estates of equal value totalling £50,000 it is only £7,500. It would, of course, be unfortunate if both husband and wife died within a short while of each other, as two lots of duty might then have to be paid instead of one, though some relief is available in those circumstances. But the principle anyway is clear.

Life assurance does not enter directly into a transaction of this kind, but it can help indirectly. First, it can make it possible for the donor to manage on a smaller amount of capital through purchase of an annuity yielding a much higher income net of tax. Secondly, it can enable the donee to provide for the duty payable if the donor dies within seven years of making his gift (*see* Plans XXXI and XXXII).

Future Retirement

For many people, the problem of providing for their retirement is at least partially solved for them by membership of a pension scheme. Whether or not they contribute directly to the scheme, the broad effect is that part of what they earn is set aside and accumulated in an insurance or other fund for payment later. A good scheme will provide pension benefits commensurate with the level of income in the years immediately preceding retirement, but the majority fall short of this standard. Many people join a good pension scheme too late to obtain the full benefit of it. People in this position, and all those whose employment is not pensionable, have to rely for the future at least partly on what they can afford to set aside from their own income year by year. The principle involved is exactly the same, although in practice better results can be achieved when pensions are funded collectively.

There are roughly three ways in which a person can provide himself with a pension by his own initiative.

Method I (Private Endowment Policy)

As explained in Chapter 3, privately-purchased annuities, as distinct from pensions provided under approved retirement benefit schemes, receive advantageous tax treatment in that the portion representing capital will be paid free of tax and only the portion representing interest will be taxable. In the case of an annuity purchased by a man at the age of 65 payable for a minimum period of five years and the remainder of life, the taxable interest content will be unlikely to exceed one-third of the total annuity. Such an annuity can be purchased by the sum assured and bonuses at maturity under a with-profit endowment assurance. The policy can be obtained with the benefit of a guaranteed annuity rate at maturity, so that the maximum sum which has to be accumulated to provide a given amount of pension is known in advance. If, at retirement, it is possible to secure a better rate, full advantage can be taken of the improvement.

The term of the policy will depend on the desired retirement age. Different types of annuity guarantee can usually be obtained. A popular choice is an annuity payable monthly in advance for a guaranteed period, usually five years and for life thereafter. At retirement, the sum assured can be exchanged for a single life annuity, or for a reduced annuity payable while the assured and his wife are alive and continuing on the life of the survivor for an equal or reduced amount.

Any person can use this method of retirement provision and claim relief against income tax on the premiums he pays within the limits described in Chapter 3. Its chief advantage is its flexibility and the fact that it is free of the restrictions imposed on the other methods considered below. For example, the policy can be assigned and used as security for a loan; it can be surrendered for cash, normally after two years' premiums have been paid; at retirement, there will be a choice between an annuity, a cash sum free of tax, or part annuity and part cash. The chief disadvantages of the method are that income tax relief is limited to two-fifths of the premiums and relief against surtax is not available. This makes it rather expensive. The other two methods are cheaper because they enable the taxpayer to save income tax and surtax on the whole of the income that is set aside. On the other hand, they are subject to certain regulations which restrict the amount of benefit that can be provided and the way in which it can be received.

This first method is particularly suitable for someone with a large investment income who can derive maximum advantage from buying his pension in the form of a purchased life annuity at retirement.

Method II ('Top Hat' Scheme)

This requires the co-operation of an employer. It is not, therefore, available to self-employed persons or controlling directors (who directly or indirectly control more than 5 per cent of the voting shares of a director-controlled company). Where circumstances make it available, it is probably the best method of all, and can be used by a person who is not already included in a superannuation scheme or, if included, wishes to supplement his benefits up to the maximum the Inland Revenue will allow. The method requires that the taxpayer, with the agreement of his employer, gives up part of his remuneration and the employer pays an equivalent sum as premiums to an endowment or other policy to provide benefits on retirement at a specified age. The company's undertaking to pay the premium must not be made dependent on the reduction in the employee's or director's salary. The two transactions must be kept quite separate from one another, otherwise the employee might find that his personal liability for tax on the salary he gave up persisted, in addition to his incurring a charge for tax on the premiums paid by the employer. This means that if the salary is included in a formal contract or service agreement the document evidencing this must be amended, but there is no reason why a contract of service should not be negotiated in the first instance to provide the employee with a specified salary *and* the benefit of a 'Top Hat' scheme.

The terms of the scheme are often expressed in a letter exchanged between the employee and the company and such a letter is adequate to meet the requirements of the Inland Revenue for approval of the scheme under S.388 of the Income Tax Act, 1952. Alternatively, there may be a set of rules in force which the company has adopted to cover similar arrangements for other directors or employees. Care must be taken in drafting such documents. If it is desired legally to protect the rights of the parties in circumstances where they might otherwise be open to question, for example, the company's liquidation, it is safer to establish the scheme by executing a trust deed with trustees, setting out the terms and conditions on which the scheme will be operated and the trust in which the benefits will be held.

The effect of approval under S.388 of the Act is that the employer's premiums will be allowed as a trading expense, the employee will not be taxed on these premiums and the pension will be taxed as earned income in his hands. An important requirement of S.388 approval is that the main benefit provided by the scheme must be a pension for life on retirement but, in practice, the Inland Revenue allows up to 25 per cent of the benefits payable in respect of the employee, including benefits to which he is entitled from any other retirement benefit scheme to which the employer has contributed, to be commuted for a tax-free lump sum. In addition, they allow substantial benefits in the form of capital sums and/or pensions to widows or dependants.

The value of the lump sum benefit at retirement is obvious. In effect, it represents part of remuneration which, had it been received at the time, would have been taxed, but by being set aside and accumulated in an endowment policy emerges tax free at the time of retirement. (Here the proverb is reversed and a bird in the bush is worth two in the hand.) It should be noted that the proportion of the 'Top Hat' benefits that can be taken in this form is not necessarily restricted to 25 per cent. If the employed person is a member of another scheme to which his employer contributes, and the pension to which he is entitled from that scheme cannot be commuted, he will then be able to commute a correspondingly larger part of his 'Top Hat' pension. It is quite possible in these circumstances that the whole of the 'Top Hat' pension could be taken as a tax-free lump sum.

This type of arrangement is also very favourable for estate duty, because the terms of the arrangement can be so drawn that the employer has discretion as to the application of the policy moneys payable on death. Provided the employer has power to exercise this discretion (and does so), because there is more than one possible beneficiary in favour of whom his discretionary powers can be exercised at the date of death, no liability to duty is likely to arise.

There is a limit on the amount of benefits that can be provided under any approved superannuation or retirement benefit scheme. Approval is not normally given under S.388 if the total pension (including pension from any other scheme of the employer) exceeds two-thirds of the employee's remuneration at retirement (salary in the last year, plus fluctuating emoluments averaged over the three preceding years), and this is scaled down where less than 20 years' service will have been completed at the time of retirement and/or there are retained benefits from previous employment or service as a controlling director. But, in any event, a pension of one-sixtieth of final remuneration for each year of service with the employer up to 40 years can be taken as the minimum that will be approved according to present practice.

It is customary for insurance companies to offer better premium rates and surrender values for policies issued in connection with 'Top Hat' schemes, and some of these policies, though they appear to be endowment assurance, are really combinations of deferred annuities and term assurance. This combination sometimes produces a better result when the different tax treatment of a company's ordinary annuity fund and life fund works in favour of the former. Such policies are often called 'ten-to-one' because the sum payable at death is ten times the pension guaranteed. In comparing the respective value of different 'Top Hat' policies, however, it is necessary to consider which is the more important, the guaranteed pension or its equivalent in cash, and this will depend partly, though by no means wholly, on the proportion which the employee himself can receive in cash.

An example of the 'Top Hat' method of providing for retirement is given in Chapter 17.

Method III (Self-employed Deferred Annuity)

This method is open to those who are not in pensionable employment, including controlling directors excluded from 'Top Hat' provision, the self-employed generally and those who, whilst they are employed persons, are not included in a retirement benefits scheme. Under S.22 of the Finance Act, 1956, they are allowed relief of income tax and surtax on premiums paid to approved deferred annuity policies as set out in Chapter 3. In this case, the regulations apply in the opposite way to those governing 'Top Hat' schemes and it is the amount of premium, not the amount of benefit, which is restricted. No lump sums can be taken, except a return of contributions with interest to the personal representatives of the contributor on death. But annuities can be provided for a widow or dependant. In certain important respects, therefore, this method of providing for retirement has less to offer the taxpayer. On the other hand, insurance companies help out by offering extremely flexible contracts which enable the contributor to vary his premium each year according to his earnings, or to withhold it altogether. This freedom of payment is obviously of great advantage to a person whose earnings fluctuate considerably, as it enables him to vary his premium in accordance with his tax liability from year to year. Each such premium secures a corresponding annuity payable at the agreed age, normally restricted to between 60 and 70. With-profit contracts are available from most companies and a few companies issue equity-linked contracts as described in Chapter 7. On the estate duty side, the Act specially provides that where a widow's annuity is payable it will always be treated as non-aggregable. Examples of these retirement annuity policies are given in Chapter 18.

In summary, it is open to anyone, regardless of the terms of his employment or the amount of his earnings, to provide for his retirement by taking out a life assurance policy and buying an annuity with the proceeds, which will only be taxed on the relatively small interest content. But only two-fifths of the premium cost will qualify for tax relief and no relief will be allowed against surtax. The 'Top Hat' scheme is probably the best method of all because at least a quarter of the proceeds of the policy can be dealt with as above, and to this is added full income tax and surtax relief on the annual outlay. But the regulations governing the scheme are stringent. The retirement annuity is most valuable to those who pay surtax on fluctuating earnings. For professional people, a combination of methods I and III is very often a sensible choice.

Present Income

For someone who has the necessary capital, the purchase of an annuity often provides a simple and effective means of increasing income. A temporary annuity coupled with an endowment policy can be used to good effect at a comparatively young age, and for an older person a life annuity will usually substantially improve income (*see* Chapter 19, Plans XXVII–XXIX). But those who, on retirement, lack capital and cannot manage comfortably on their pension or other income, present a special problem. Usually, a home is the last thing people willingly give up and even if this is sold to purchase an annuity, future rent will have to be met from the annuity payments.

There are two possible solutions to their problem. One is to raise a mortgage, and at least one insurance company is now willing to grant loans on a private residence to enable owners to purchase an immediate single or joint life annuity. The scheme applies to men over 65 and women over 60. The sum made available from the insurance company to purchase an annuity is 50 per cent to 60 per cent of the value of the property, subject to a minimum loan of £1,000 and a maximum of £5,000. At the time of writing, interest is charged at 6½ per cent.

The alternative solution is to take advantage of a new scheme which offers a ready-made way of converting house ownership into income with the minimum of inconvenience and no loss of occupation rights. The company which has been specially set up to operate the scheme purchases the house and, in return, provides the vendor with a fixed income for life and a life tenancy in the home at a nominal rent. Husband and wife then retain undisputed right to their home and a guaranteed income for as long as they live (*see* Chapter 19, Plan XXX). This proposition should however be approached with great caution.

17

Buying a Pension (Employed Person)

PLAN XXIII

A senior executive, aged 50 next birthday, earns a salary of £4,000 a year and commissions averaging an additional £1,000. He wishes to provide himself with a pension on retirement at the age of 65, and a lump sum for his dependants should he die beforehand. He is not entitled to any existing pension provision.

As explained in Chapter 16, the essence of this plan, colloquially called 'Top Hat', is the acceptance on the part of the employee of a reduction in earnings and the application by the employer of an amount equivalent to this reduction as premiums to an endowment or similar policy. The executive then agrees to forgo, say, the first £500 of his commissions, and the employer consents to pay a like amount each year to an endowment with-profits policy to which a guaranteed annuity option is attached. It is sufficient for tax purposes if the terms and conditions governing the arrangement are set out in a letter from the employer to the employee, which the employee acknowledges. Alternatively, if similar arrangements are to be made for other personnel, the employer can adopt a set of rules sufficiently flexible to cover the provision of different levels of benefit according to their separate requirements. The provisions of the arrangement or scheme are drafted so as to secure the approval of the Inland Revenue under S.388 (1), Income Tax Act, 1952. The insurance company, or brokers, will supply a suitable draft of the form of documentation required and undertake the necessary negotiations with the Inland Revenue to secure this approval. The effect of approval is that, for tax purposes, the premiums will be allowed as an expense to the employer and will not be added back to the employee's remuneration.

As a result of this procedure, the employer is in exactly the same position so far as his total outgoings are concerned, but the employee is relieved of tax on the top slice of his earnings and obtains the benefit of the gross investment of these earnings when he comes to retire. At the risk of being repetitious, it must be emphasized that for the reduction in earnings to be effective for tax purposes it has to be an absolute reduction and not one which is conditional upon the employer paying an equivalent amount in premiums, and it follows that anything dependent on the employee's earnings (e.g., a pension under another scheme of the employer, if such exists) must be based on his reduced earnings.

'Top Hat' Policy

Male, aged 50 next birthday
Normal retirement date: sixty-fifth birthday

BENEFITS:

(1) On death in service before normal retirement date a capital sum of *plus* bonuses on this sum	£6,825
(2) On retirement at normal retirement date	
either	
(*a*) an estimated pension of	£992 per annum
or	
(*b*) an estimated lump sum of	£2,602
and an estimated pension of	£744 per annum
The pension is payable monthly in advance for five years in any event and for life thereafter.	

COST:

Annual premium for 15 years	£500
Less: income tax saved on £500	161
Net effective loss of earnings	£339
Total net loss of earnings £339 × 15	£5,085

Notes:

(1) Inland Revenue approval is dependent on the pension not exceeding the maximum currently laid down. In this case, assuming the executive had already completed five years' service with the employer prior to the commencement of the arrangement, his total pensionable service to normal retirement date would be 20 years, and assuming that he had not in the past held a position as a controlling director and had no retained benefits from previous employment, the maximum approvable pension at normal retirement date would be two-thirds of his reduced remuneration.

(2) The estimated pension shown is calculated by applying the minimum annuity rate guaranteed in the policy to the estimated cash value of the policy at maturity (basic sum assured plus bonuses estimated at 70*s* per cent per annum simple). Up to one-quarter of this benefit can be taken by the employee as a lump sum (unless he is in serious ill-health when, exceptionally, the whole of it can be commuted) and the balance must be applied by the employer to secure a non-commutable pension on the employee's life, though not necessarily with the company underwriting the policy. If, when the pension becomes payable, the employer can obtain a higher rate of annuity than that guaranteed, the employee will benefit from the improvement, so long as the increased pension does not exceed the maximum the Inland Revenue will approve in relation to the employee's final remuneration. (There are various ways in which final remuneration can be calculated, one of which is salary in the last year before retirement, plus commissions and other fluctuating emoluments averaged over the three preceding years.) (*Note:* directors' fees cannot be included in pensionable remuneration.) At the present time, the pension shown in the example could be improved at current annuity rates by approximately 17 per cent.

(3) If the employee wants to receive his benefit wholly as pension it will still pay him to take the maximum amount permitted in cash and then re-invest this in an annuity, since the annuity so purchased will qualify as a purchased life annuity and will not be regarded as having been provided from a retirement benefit scheme. The capital element will therefore escape tax, but the balance of the annuity will be taxed as unearned income and the pension from the scheme will qualify for earned income relief.

(4) On death in service, it is normally arranged that the proceeds of the policy shall be payable by the employer to one or more dependants or relatives of the employee, as the employer at his sole discretion may decide. On this basis, because power of disposal is taken out of the assured's hands, the benefit is normally free of estate duty, and

this is an important secondary advantage of a 'Top Hat' scheme. The employee will usually indicate to whom he would like the benefit payable in the event of his death and the employer will usually comply with the employee's known wishes, but is not bound to do so. If the employer does not exercise his power within a specified time, it is usually provided that the policy moneys are then held by the employer in trust for the benefit of statutory next-of-kin or personal representatives.

(5) At retirement, the employee can elect to give up part of his pension so that his wife or other dependant may receive a pension after his death. The widow's or dependant's pension must not exceed the pension remaining on the life of the employee. Provided that this election, once made, is irrevocable, it is the present practice of the estate duty office to regard the widow's pension as being an interest which arises at the time the election is made and not at the time it becomes payable by virtue of survivorship, with the result that S.2(1)(*d*) of the Finance Act, 1894, does not apply and the pension escapes duty. But this has not always been the position.

(6) The arrangement will provide for early and late retirement with appropriate adjustment of the benefits. It frequently happens that an employee stays on after normal retirement date, when the policy matures for payment. Although the usual practice is for the insurance company to hold the policy moneys until actual retirement takes place, there is no reason why the employer should not do so himself with the prospect of getting a better return which can be passed on to the employee in the form of an improved late retirement pension.

(7) If the employee leaves service and has indirectly contributed to the arrangement by an adjustment in remuneration as envisaged here, he will normally be entitled, on leaving, to the paid-up policy benefits, which must be taken at normal retirement date or such earlier date (but normally not earlier than ten years before normal retirement date) as he retires from remunerative employment. If this right is not embodied in the rules governing the arrangement, it can be dealt with in a separate letter to the employee. The policy will normally be assigned to the employee and he will be able to maintain the full benefits by paying future premiums himself. In this event, the policy will be appropriately endorsed to the effect that the proportionate part of the benefits secured by his own premiums is free of the restrictions applicable to the arrangement.

* * *

In the above example, it was assumed that the employee was not entitled to a pension from any other retirement benefit scheme of the employer. However, it is often the case that an executive is a member of his company's superannuation fund, which provides a non-commutable pension, and wishes to use the method indicated above to supplement this pension. If, in the example, the executive was entitled to a superannuation fund pension of one-sixtieth of final salary (excluding commissions) for each year of service, his present expected pension from this source, assuming no future changes in basic salary, would be twenty-sixtieths of £4,000, which equals £1,333. The commutation position would then be that, provided not less than three-quarters of the aggregate pension was received as pension, the balance from the 'Top Hat' scheme could be encashed. This would work out as follows:

(*a*) Non-commutable pension from fund	£1,333
(*b*) Pension from this arrangement	992
Aggregate pension	£2,325

One-quarter of aggregate pension is $\frac{£2,325}{4}$ = £581

Cash value of this is £6,096

In these circumstances, it will be seen that the whole of the net cost of the arrangement to the employee is repaid by the lump sum at retirement, and to this is added over £1,000 estimated tax-free capital profit and an estimated residual pension of £411. In addition, the employee has enjoyed substantial life assurance cover at no cost and free of estate duty.

Other Considerations

Increases in Pension after Retirement

Once an employee has retired the employer can, if the circumstances warrant, take independent action to improve an employee's pension but is unlikely to do so if the arrangement was that the pension would be wholly financed by the employee on the basis described. The question of inflation after retirement is therefore one which should be considered in advance. Since the war the average rate of currency inflation has been about 3½ per cent per annum and recent signs are that this is likely to increase rather than decrease. The table below shows the effect of inflation on the purchasing power of a pension which had a value of £1,000 at age 65.

Rate of inflation	*Pension at 65*	*Approximate value at 75*	*Approximate value at 85*
3½ per cent	£1,000	£708 19*s* 0*d*	£502 12*s* 0*d*

At age 65 a man's expectation of life is approximately 14 years. Naturally, some will die earlier but conversely, some may live to age 90 or more. The most satisfactory method of dealing with this problem is to purchase a pension which increases automatically each year after retirement. The annual rate of increase allowed is 2½ per cent per annum compound of the total benefit being paid in pension form, provided that the aggregate increase does not at any time exceed the increase in the Ministry of Labour's index of retail prices since the date of retirement. Fortunately, in the case of a fall in the index, the Inland Revenue will not insist on an increase already given being withdrawn or reduced.

To illustrate this let us assume that the maximum pension approvable by Revenue on the basis of current remuneration is £1,000. To provide a fixed pension of this amount the sum assured required is £10,000. One-quarter of this can be taken in cash, leaving a residual pension of £750. The pension of £750 can be set up on the basis that it increases at 2½ per cent per annum compound for an additional sum assured of £1,500 making £11,500 in all. This additional sum assured can be paid to dependants in the event of death but the Inland Revenue will not allow it to be included in the amount available for commutation at retirement.

Widow's Pension on Death after Retirement

The Inland Revenue will allow, in addition to the maximum approvable pension on the employee's life, provision for a separate widow's pension of up to one-half the employee's pension, payable as from the date of his death. The widow's pension may also be set up to increase at 2½ per cent compound per annum as from normal retiring date. This can be provided by taking out a deferred reversionary annuity as part of the 'Top Hat' arrangement, or by setting up an additional sum assured with a guaranteed reversionary annuity rate attached to it. In the latter event the amount which can be paid to the employee's dependants on death in service may have to be restricted. A guide to the maximum pension and death in service benefits currently acceptable to the Inland Revenue is given below.

Inland Revenue Limits on Benefit

Pension

The maximum pension which the Inland Revenue will allow for 20 years' service or more is two-thirds of final salary. The Inland Revenue allow bonuses, commission, etc. (but not directors' fees) to be included in 'final salary' provided that such earnings are averaged over the last three years or such shorter period as they may have been paid. (*See* Table 1 on page 148.)

These are maximum pensions. In certain circumstances lower limits will apply, for example if there are retained pension rights or contributions have been refunded from an approved pension scheme in previous employment.

Death in service benefit

The maximum death in service benefits are normally as follows:

(*a*) £7,500.
or (*b*) If between £7,500 and £25,000, the greater of:
  (i) 7 × remuneration.
  (ii) The capital value of the pension.
and (*c*) If over £25,000 the capital value of the pension.

Where the death in service benefit is not in the form of a capital sum, e.g. widow's or children's annuity, a notional capital value is given to it in order to determine the amount that will be approved.

TABLE 1

Years of service that can be completed by normal retirement date	*Maximum pension expressed as* (i) *60 ths*	(ii) *percentages*
1	1	1·67
2	2	3·33
3	3	5·0
4	4	6·67
5	5	8·33
6	6	10·00
7	7	11·67
8	8	13·33
9	10	16·67
10	12	20·00
11	14	23·33
12	16	26·67
13	18	30·00
14	21	35·00
15	24	40·00
16	27	45·00
17	30	50·00
18	33	55·00
19	36	60·00
20 or over	40	66·67

18

Buying a Pension (Self-employed and Others)

Introductory

The method of buying a pension illustrated here is to take out annuity contracts under S.22 and 23 of the Finance Act, 1956. As explained in Chapter 16, these contracts are available to self-employed persons and others who cannot take advantage of the method described in the previous chapter, and also to employees not already pensionable. Thus they are suitable for professional men in practice (for example, accountants, architects, barristers, solicitors and surveyors), individuals and partners in business which are not companies (for example, craftsmen, farmers and shopkeepers), controlling directors of companies and employees who will not benefit under pension schemes set up by their employers.

Persons in pensionable employment who are also engaged in some occupation which is non-pensionable, (e.g., doctors who have a part-time salaried post and carry on a practice), can use this method of buying a pension in respect of income obtained from the non-pensionable occupation.

Premiums will be allowed in full as a deduction from earnings in the computation of the assessable income for income tax and surtax purposes, subject to the conditions set out in Chapter 3. The pensions payable will be taxable as income but will qualify for earned income relief.

Insurance companies have devised special contracts to meet the requirements of those eligible to take advantage of these tax reliefs. A selection of these is shown in the following three plans, which can be used as the basis of a retirement scheme, both by those with stable and those with fluctuating incomes.

Plan XXIV is suitable primarily for those with a relatively

stable income who feel able to commit themselves to a systematic plan of saving for retirement and can take full advantage of a free choice of retirement age.

Plan XXV describes a method suitable for those with sharply fluctuating incomes who find it impracticable to plan too far ahead, and who are not likely to derive the maximum tax advantages on a fixed premium. It is also very suitable for use in conjunction with Plan XXVI.

Plan XXVI provides benefits which are not fixed and guaranteed but linked to the market value of a fund invested mainly in ordinary shares.

Pension age.—The pension can commence at any time chosen by the contributor between his sixtieth and seventieth birthdays. The pension can be drawn before the age of 60 if the contributor becomes incapable from illness or accident from carrying on his profession or occupation. In certain ocupations where it is customary to retire before 60, the Inland Revenue may agree to the pension starting earlier than this age but not before 50.

How the pension is paid.—The pensions are normally payable monthly or quarterly for life, with the option of a guaranteed minimum term of five or ten years.

Widow's or dependant's pension.—At the time his pension starts, the contributor can decide to allocate part of the pension secured on his own life to provide a pension payable to his widow or other dependant after his death, and in the normal way this option is not subject to evidence of health. The pension payable to the widow or other dependant must not exceed the amount of the pension remaining payable to the contributor. The terms of this conversion option are normally guaranteed in the policy.

On the death of the policyholder, the value of the pension to the widow or dependant will be subject to estate duty but on a non-aggregable basis. In other words, the rate of duty will be determined by reference to the value of the widow's pension itself, together with the value of any other benefit to which the widow may be entitled under other life assurance policies effected in trust on the policyholder's life.

Tax Treatment of Pension

Pension payments, whether to the policyholder or to his widow or other dependant, will rank as earned income for tax purposes.

Death before Retirement

In the event of the death of the contributor before payment of the pension starts, all premiums paid are returnable (with interest usually at 4 per cent; or without interest, in which event an appropriate allowance for mortality is made in the premium rates). The return on death will be subject to estate duty at the rate appropriate to the whole of the policyholder's main estate.

As an alternative to this, most insurance companies offer to endorse the policy so that the amount credited to the policyholder at death is used to purchase an annuity for the policyholder's widow or other dependant approved by the Inland Revenue, and this benefit will be non-aggregable.

Supplementary Life Assurance

If the contributor should die within a few years after starting to pay premiums to the plans illustrated below, the amount returned to his estate by way of premium and interest, or the annuity payable to his widow or dependant, would be comparatively small, but in later years the death return would be considerable. In view of this, most insurance companies offer a form of decreasing term assurance in conjunction with these contracts, which bridges the gap and brings the total amount at early death up to a pre-determined figure.

PLAN XXIV

A man aged 40 next birthday has an earned income of £2,500 a year until he is 45 and thereafter his earnings increase to £3,000. He decides that he will pay each year until retirement the maximum qualifying premium which, in his case, is £250 for five years, increasing thereafter to £300. The approximate amount of benefit he can expect to receive from a good with-profits contract, assuming current bonus levels continue, is set out below.

Policy Description: Chapter 7

DEFERRED ANNUITIES WITH PROFITS BY ANNUAL PREMIUMS

Amount of pension	*Guaranteed*	*Estimated*
Assuming retirement at		
Age 65	£804 2*s* 8*d*	£1,506 18*s* 0*d*
Age 67	£963 5*s* 8*d*	£1,904 2*s* 8*d*
Age 70	£1,273 13*s* 8*d*	£2,714 1*s* 8*d*

The figures quoted are that of a company which guarantees at the outset the amounts of pension, subject to increase by bonus additions payable at all retirement ages from 60 to 70. As this example is for an annual premium contract, it should be appreciated that the rate used for the increased annual premium paid five years hence cannot be guaranteed in advance.

Widow's Pension

If he elects at retirement to allocate part of his pension to provide an annuity payable after his death to his wife (who is three years younger), the amount of the widow's annuity for each £100 of pension given up would be:

Assuming retirement at	*Guaranteed*
Age 65	£244 0*s* 0*d*
Age 67	£231 0*s* 0*d*
Age 70	£215 0*s* 0*d*

Death before Pension Starts

If he dies before retirement, the benefit could be either a return of all premiums paid or an annuity to his widow. The figures set out below illustrate these alternative benefits on the assumption that annuity rates (based on present levels) are maintained and that his wife is three years younger.

Age at death	*Number of annual premiums paid*	*Return of premiums*		*Widow's annuity per annum*
49	10	£2,750	OR	£194 4s od
54	15	£4,250		£318 11s od
59	20	£5,750		£464 15s od

PLAN XXV

A man aged 55 next birthday in 1965, whose income is liable to fluctuate sharply from year to year, decides he will set aside each year for retirement as much as he can afford in the light of his actual earnings for that year. Assuming that his earnings and the premiums paid are as shown in the table below, and that his pension is built up by the application of these premiums to secure single premium deferred annuities with profits, the benefits secured at the age of 65 would be approximately as shown.

Policy Description: Chapter 7

DEFERRED ANNUITIES WITH PROFITS BY SINGLE PREMIUMS

Year of assessment	*Earnings*	*Single premium paid*	*Guaranteed annuity*	*Estimated annuity*
	£	£	£ *s* *d*	£ *s* *d*
1	3,500	450	61 8 0	79 16 0
2	3,000	350	46 0 0	58 8 0
3	5,500	650	82 11 0	102 7 0
4	7,000	850	104 2 0	125 19 0
5	3,000	350	41 6 0	48 15 0
6	2,000	200	22 16 0	26 4 0
7	4,000	500	54 15 0	61 6 0
8	3,500	450	47 5 0	51 10 0
9	5,000	600	60 18 0	64 11 0
10	4,000	400	39 8 0	40 12 0
		4,800	560 9 0	659 8 0

Note: In practice, it might be decided to secure non-profit annuities in the last three or four years with equally good or better results.

PLAN XXVI

The two preceding plans provide benefits which are basically fixed and guaranteed. Some people may prefer an alternative form of contract which, whilst securing the normal tax reliefs, will enable them to enjoy the benefits which in favourable circumstances can be derived from investment in ordinary shares. The variable annuity plan illustrated below is designed to meet this need, but it is considered suitable only as a method of supplementing regular contributions to the two preceding plans for someone with a fairly substantial income to spend.

Introduction

All premiums are paid to a special fund which is normally invested almost entirely in ordinary shares. The benefits available to the policyholder are expressed in units, the values of which fluctuate in accordance with the experience of the fund. There is thus no fixed guaranteed benefit as in a conventional contract. The special fund, which is known as the Variable Annuity Fund, has been created solely to provide annuities which are subject to fluctuation in this manner, and it is administered separately from the other funds of the insurance company in question. It does not constitute a trust fund for the policyholders as beneficiaries, but its value from time to time is a prime factor in the calculation by the company of the benefits under the plan. This plan is, therefore, fundamentally different from one in which the benefits are linked to the value of units in a unit trust outside the control of the insurance company.

Payment of First Premium

On payment of the first premium the contributor is allotted a number of units equivalent to the premium paid. These units are known as accumulation units and the number allotted, which depends on the gross value of the units at the time, is a measure of the benefits which will ultimately be available by way of pension or death benefit in return for the premium.

Investment of Funds

All premiums paid are carried to the accumulation account of the Variable Annuity Fund and invested at the discretion of the company. The company can invest the funds in whatever manner appears to it to be best, but the general intention is that it should invest almost exclusively in high-grade ordinary shares.

Dividends and Interest

Dividend and interest income earned by the assets representing the accumulation account is carried to that account. The whole of the dividend and interest income of the Variable Annuity Fund is, under present law, exempt from United Kingdom income tax, so that tax deducted at source from this income is normally reclaimed in full. The fund is, however, subject to the same limitations as any other exempt body, in that it is only able to reclaim tax which has been effectively received by the United Kingdom tax authorities in respect of that income.

Value of Accumulation Units

From time to time, the company determines the net value of the accumulation unit on an equitable basis, having regard to the current market value of the assets representing the accumulation account and the number of accumulation units outstanding. Accretions to the account by way of dividends and interest thus tend to increase the value of the accumulation unit, though from time to time this tendency may be more than offset by a fall in value due to depreciation in the market value of the assets representing the account. The net value of the accumulation unit is used for determining the amount payable to the estates of those policyholders who die before the commencement of their annuities and also the amounts available for the provision of annuities. The gross value of the accumulation unit, i.e., the amount which has to be paid by way of premium at any time to secure one accumulation unit, is the current net value of the unit, increased by an equitable amount to allow for expenses. As each additional premium is paid, a certificate is issued to the contributor showing the number of accumulation units secured by the premium in question and also the total of the accumulation units secured to date.

Death before the Pension Starts

If the contributor dies before his pension starts, his estate receives an amount equal to the current net value of the accumulation units at the date of his death.

Choice of Variable or Fixed Annuity

When the contributor elects to receive his pension he may select either:

(*i*) a variable annuity, i.e., an annuity the amount of which will vary from time to time in accordance with the experience of the fund

or

(*ii*) a fixed annuity, i.e., an annuity providing a constant sterling amount each year

or

(*iii*) a combination of (*i*) and (*ii*).

The amount available for providing the annuity is the total net value at the date of election of all the accumulation units secured by the policy. This total value may be split in accordance with (*iii*) above to provide both a variable and a fixed annuity.

Variable Annuity

If the policyholder selects a variable annuity the net value of his accumulation units (or the appropriate part of that value, if option (*iii*) is exercised) is transferred from the accumulation account to the annuity account of the variable annuity fund and is converted into an annuity on an equitable basis determined by the company's actuary. The annuity is then expressed in terms of annuity units on the basis of the then current value of the annuity unit, so that the amount actually to be received in future by the policyholder may fluctuate in accordance with the experience of the fund, which is reflected in the value of the annuity unit.

Value of Annuity Units

The value of the annuity unit is calculated from time to time on an equitable basis, and is such that, in the opinion of the company's actuary, the funds held in respect of the variable annuity account are, on the basis of market prices and dividends current at the date of calculation, sufficient to meet all the variable annuities included in the account throughout the remainder of their currency. If all the annuitants should die, the balance in the variable annuity account would be transferred back to the accumulation account.

The value of the annuity unit tends to rise if either the market price of the securities in the fund or the rate of dividend declared on those securities increases. Equally, it tends to fall if market prices or dividends decline. It also tends to rise if the mortality of the annuitants is heavier than was assumed, and to fall if the mortality is lighter than assumed.

Fixed Annuity

If the policyholder selects a fixed annuity, the net value of his accumulation units (or the appropriate part of that value, if option (*iii*) is exercised) is transferred out of the variable annuity fund entirely and converted into a fixed annuity on equitable terms. (For various reasons, including the taxation of the company's funds, the annuity offered may not be based on the company's published immediate annuity rates at the time.)

Policy Description: Chapter 7

VARIABLE ANNUITY

No forecast can be given as to the future experience of the fund, but it is assumed for the purposes of this example that dividend and interest earnings each year will amount to 4 per cent of the current market value of the assets, and that the mortality of the fund's annuitants will be in accordance with current published tables for this class of life. It is assumed that the contributor pays a premium of £100 each year to secure a pension at the age of 65, payable in quarterly instalments in advance for the remainder of his life, but with no guaranteed period.

If it is assumed that the market value of the assets of the fund will appreciate sufficiently to cover the company's investment expenses (i.e., brokerage and stamp duties), but otherwise will remain steady, the annuities payable will be as follows:

Age when contributions commence	35	40	45	50	55	60
Pension at 65	£490	£366	£263	£178	£107	£48

If the policyholder were to die exactly at the age 65, but before electing to take his pension, the benefit payable would be as follows:

Age when contributions commence	35	40	45	50	55	60
Death benefit at 65	£5,293	£3,955	£2,845	£1,924	£1,160	£526

If it is assumed that the market value of the assets of the fund will appreciate sufficiently to cover the company's investment expenses and to show, in addition, an increase in value of 2 per cent each year, the annuities at the age of 65 will start at the following amounts:

Age when contributions commence	35	40	45	50	55	60
Pension at 65	£703	£491	£332	£211	£120	£51

After 65, the amount of the annuity will, on this assumption, increase continuously at the rate of 2 per cent per annum so that each £100 of annuity at the age of 65 will become £110 at the age of 70 and £121 at the age of 75.

If the policyholder were to die exactly at 65, but before electing to take his pension, the benefit payable would be as follows:

Age when contributions commence	35	40	45	50	55	60
Death benefit at 65	£7,591	£5,305	£3,580	£2,279	£1,298	£558

Conclusion

It will be seen that, in this type of plan, the insurance company bears no risk in connection with the operation of the fund. The whole of this risk is borne by the policyholders, who benefit from a favourable experience but suffer if the experience is adverse. Before his pension commences, the policyholder in effect bears the investment risk (i.e., the risk of fluctuations in dividends and capital values) while after the commencement of his pension, if he elects to take this in the form of a variable annuity, he bears both the investment risk and the mortality risk (i.e., the risk that annuitants will live longer than has been assumed by the insurance company).

19

Buying an Annuity

PLAN XXVII

A man, aged 40, has investments worth £100,000 and an earned income of £3,000. He wishes to increase his spendable income by re-investing part of his capital to secure a higher tax-free yield, with an opportunity of reviewing the position at a later date.

As explained in Chapter 15, purchase of an annuity for life, although it would improve immediate income, would be foolish at so young an age. It is suggested, therefore, that £50,000 be spent on a temporary life annuity which would cease at the end of 15 years or on earlier death. At the same time, a with-profit endowment assurance is taken out to mature in 15 years' time or on previous death, so as to replace the capital spent on the annuity.

TEMPORARY LIFE ANNUITY PLUS ENDOWMENT ASSURANCE WITH PROFITS

Male, aged 40

Annuity

Purchase price	£50,000
Gross annuity payable for a maximum of 15 years	£5,250
(Capital element)	(£3,423)
(Annual amount assessable for tax)	(£1,827)

The annuity would be payable in half-yearly instalments, the first payment being made six months after the date of purchase. The annuity would continue throughout the lifetime of the annuitant, the last payment being that due immediately preceding death or at the end of fifteen years, whichever is earlier.

Endowment assurance

Sum assured payable at the end of 15 years or previous death	£35,000
Estimated bonus additions, assuming an average rate of bonus of 70*s* per cent per annum simple	18,375
Total estimated sum at maturity	£53,375
Annual premium (payable in half-yearly instalments)	£2,500

POSITION BEFORE EFFECTING PLAN:

Investments	£100,000
Gross income yield at 5 per cent	5,000
Earned income	3,000
Total gross income	8,000
Estimated income tax and surtax	3,910
Net income	£4,090

POSITION AFTER EFFECTING PLAN:

Initial capital expended on the plan:

Purchase price of annuity		£50,000
First half-yearly premium for endowment assurance		1,250
Total expenditure		£51,250
Remaining investments		£48,750
Gross income yield at 5 per cent		2,437
Earned income		3,000
Gross annuity		5,250
Total gross income		£10,687
Capital content of annuity	£3,423	
Taxable income	£7,264	
Estimated income tax and surtax (after allowing for life assurance relief)		3,170
Net income		7,517
Less premium for endowment assurance		2,500
Net spendable income		£5,017

Summary

The suggested plan has increased net income by *£927 per annum*. At the end of 15 years, the endowment assurance would mature to replace the capital which has been spent. Assuming that bonuses accumulate at 70*s* per cent per annum simple, there would be a capital gain, tax free, of £2,125.

PLAN XXVIII

The only private income of a lady, aged 75, is £150 a year, derived from investments yielding 5 per cent. She has no real dependants but would like to leave something to one or two relations for them to remember her by after her death. Subject to this, she wants to increase her income by as much as possible for the rest of her life.

Immediate Annuity

She sells two-thirds of her investments in order to purchase an annuity of approximately £275 per annum, payable for her lifetime. As a result, her income is increased by £175 to £325 a year. Neither before nor after the purchase of the annuity is her income subject to tax.

After the purchase, she still retains capital investments worth £1,000 at current value.

PLAN XXIX

A retired person aged 70 and his wife aged 67 review their finances. Apart from the State pension and a pension arising from previous employment of £300 per annum, of which £200 would continue as a widow's pension, their income consists of dividends of £400 gross per annum on savings valued at £8,000. On the present scale of taxation, the net income while both live amounts to £858 per annum and, after the husband's death, his widow will be left with a net annual income of £673. They would like to make an immediate gift of £2,000 to assist their son and daughter but they cannot afford to give up part of their income to do so.

IMMEDIATE ANNUITY PLUS REVERSIONARY ANNUITY

Male aged 70
Wife aged 67

They employ £4,000 of their savings to buy an annuity on the husband's life of £380 per annum and a reversionary annuity of the same amount on the wife's life, payable after his death. Of this, £260 is free of tax at outset, and the increased net income they get by applying this part of their capital to an annuity more than offsets the loss of income from the amount given away, viz:

(*a*) Their net income, while both are alive, is increased by £169 per annum to £1,027 per annum.
(*b*) After the husband's death, if this occurred in 5 years' time, his widow could expect her net income to be £767 per annum.
(*c*) They retain £2,000 to meet emergencies or for the wife to employ in purchasing an additional annuity later on.

PLAN XXX

A retired executive, aged 73, and his wife aged 71, own a house with a market value of £7,850. Their only source of income is a pension of £700 a year. As a result of inflation, they can no longer manage comfortably on this but lack funds to buy an annuity.

One possible solution to this problem is to raise a mortgage, and at least one insurance company at the time of writing is willing to lend the purchase price of an annuity in these circumstances up to 65 per cent of valuation. The plan illustrated here, however, involves selling the house with the right of a life tenancy at a nominal rent. It should be approached with caution and may not be suitable if there is any likelihood that, on the death of one of the partners, the widow or widower might wish to move. In these circumstances, the company will give special consideration to increasing the annuity by an appropriate amount in consideration of their obtaining immediate possession of the house, but no guarantees are given in the contract.

House Sale with Reversionary Interest

How the Plan Works

The company undertakes to purchase the house for a percentage of its market value, the percentage depending on the life expectancy of the couple. The consideration is provided in the form of a fixed annuity payable until the death of the survivor and a life tenancy of the house.

A nominal rental is charged amounting to £1 a month. This is fixed and cannot be increased. The agreement is so framed that the annuity qualifies as a privately-purchased life annuity, so that only the interest content is taxable. Up to £1,000 can be taken in cash and the annuity reduced *pro rata.*

The transfer of the property is made in complete confidence and outwardly its ownership is unchanged. A survey fee is charged on application, part of which is returned if the offer is accepted. All legal fees are paid by the company.

Male aged 73
Wife aged 71
House valued at £7,850

Annuity in consideration of sale of house, subject to life tenancy at £1 per month: £412 per annum, of which £250 is exempt from tax.

The annuity is payable monthly in arrear on the life of husband and wife until the death of the survivor.

20

Simple Estate Duty Schemes

PLAN XXXI

This makes provision for estate duty liability on a gift made within the donor's lifetime. It is assumed that the estate owner has assets of £60,000 and has a wife and two grown-up children who are the sole beneficiaries under his will. He decides to make gifts of £10,000 to each of them.

As explained in Chapter 4, the present estate duty laws provide that if the donor dies within seven years of making the gift the value of the gift as at the date of death is added back to the remainder of his estate and duty is assessed accordingly. If death occurs within four years of making the gift, the full value is added back. The proportions added back if death occurs in years five to seven are as follows:

year five	85 per cent
year six	70 per cent
year seven	40 per cent

The plan consists of a seven-year temporary assurance on the life of the donor to provide the amount of duty payable in the event of the donor's death within the period in which duty is chargeable. The policy is taken out by the wife on the life of her husband. This ensures that the policy moneys are free of duty in the event of a claim arising. It is assumed that the premium can be paid by the wife out of her own resources; otherwise it is possible that it will be added back with the principal gift for purposes of assessing the rate of duty payable. (The exemptions from the liability of gifts of duty under existing laws include gifts which are accepted by the estate duty officers as being part of the *normal* expenditure of the deceased and to have been paid out of income rather than capital, leaving sufficient income to maintain the donor's usual standard of living (*see* Chapter 4).)

The following table shows how the potential liability to duty is arrived at for the purpose of fixing the sums assured under the policy, on the assumption that the value of the estate, including the value of the gifts, remains unchanged during the period under review.

Period elapsed between date of gift and date of death	*Proportion of the gifts which is dutiable*	*Total estate for duty purposes*	*Rate of duty*	*Amount of duty on the gifts*	*Amount of duty on the main estate*
(1)	(2)	(3)	(4)	(5)	(6)
Up to 4 years	100%=£30,000	£60,000	35%	£10,500	£10,500
4 to 5 years	85%=£25,500	£55,500	35%	£8,925	£10,500
5 to 6 years	70%=£21,000	£51,000	35%	£6,795	£9,705
6 to 7 years	40%=£12,000	£42,000	28%	£3,315	£8,285

Notes: The figures in column (3) are calculated by adding back the dutiable proportion of the gifts (column (2)) to the estate of £30,000 retained by the donor.

The figures in columns (4), (5) and (6) applicable to the sixth and seventh years are adjusted for marginal relief (*see* Chapter 4).

Gift Protection Policy

Male aged 70 next birthday

Sum assured payable in the event of death

Immediately	£10,500
After one year	£10,500
After two years	£10,500
After three years	£10,500
After four years	£8,925
After five years	£6,795
After six years	£3,315
At the end of seven years	the contract comes to an end

COST:

either

Single premium of £2,446

or

Six annual premiums of £472

Note: As the policy is effected by a wife on the life of her husband, premiums are eligible for normal relief of income tax (subject to one-sixth limit) assessed on combined income of husband and wife.

PLAN XXXII

In spite of the Finance Act, 1968, it is still possible for an elderly man in reasonably good health to make an effective saving in his potential estate duty liability. This saving can be achieved by making a gift in his lifetime to the intended beneficiaries and preserving his own and his wife's income through the purchase of annuities. The gift protection policy illustrated in Plan XXXI is used to cover the liability for estate duty during the statutory period of seven years.

The example is that of a man aged 72 with a wife aged 70. Their children are grown up and they have no allowances beyond the ordinary personal allowance to set against income tax and surtax and their income is all unearned. It is assumed that the husband's estate is worth £250,000 consisting of readily realizable assets and his wife has virtually nothing. It is assumed that the husband's assets earn 5 per cent per annum gross.

In this plan, £60,000 is invested in a joint life and survivor annuity and £150,000 is given to the children who cover their estate duty liability by means of a gift protection policy on the lines illustrated in Plan XXXI. The annuity purchase price is divided into two sums which are used to purchase immediate annuities of equal amounts for husband and wife. On the death of either, the survivor's gross annuity will be doubled for the remainder of his or her lifetime. To achieve this, the husband purchases an annuity for himself and gives his wife a sufficient sum to purchase her own annuity and buy a single premium gift protection policy on his life to cover the estimated duty on the gift. As a result the duty liability is fixed at outset, subject only to legislative changes.

Immediate Annuities plus Gift Protection Policy

Male aged 72, Female aged 70

Immediate annuities

Purchase moneys	£60,000
Joint life and survivor annuity	6,732
(Capital element)	3,822
(Annual amount assessable for tax)	2,850

Gift Protection Policies

By wife	
Sum assured payable on death immediately	£24,814
Single premium	6,146
By children	
Sum assured payable on death immediately	£90,000
Single premium	22,269

POSITION BEFORE EFFECTING PLAN:

1. *Estate duty*

Total estate	£250,000
Estate duty at 60 per cent	150,000
Net estate passing to beneficiaries	£100,000

Note: If it is assumed that the bulk of the estate will be left to the wife, on passing at her death, another duty charge of 45 per cent (if capital value remains unchanged) will be levied meaning that the ultimate beneficiaries may only receive £55,000 (assuming she survived him by 5 years when no 'quick succession' relief will apply).

2. *Income*

£250,000 at 5 per cent		£12,500
Income tax	£4,972	
Surtax	3,237	8,209
Net income		£4,291

POSITION AFTER EFFECTING PLAN:

1. Estate duty

Gross estate		£250,000
Less purchase price of husband's annuity		24,789
Resulting dutiable estate		£225,211
Less gifts		
(*a*) *To wife:* annuity purchase price	£35,211	
single premium gift protection policy	6,146	£ 41,357
		£183,854
(*b*) *To children:* free capital	£127,731	
single premium gift protection policy	22,269	£150,000
Net free estate		£ 33,854

If death occurs within four years of the gifts being made a total duty charge of 60 per cent of the dutiable estate will be levied, i.e. *£135,127.*

This will be apportioned as follows:

On gift to wife 60 per cent of	£ 41,357	=	£ 24,814
On gift to beneficiaries 60 per cent of	150,000	=	90,000
On free estate 60 per cent of	33,854	=	20,313
Total			£135,127

As duty on the gifts is fully covered by the gift protection policy the net amount passing to the children if death occurs during the first four years will be:

Value of gift	£150,000	
Less: gift protection premium	22,269	£127,731
Free estate	£ 33,854	
Less: duty at 60 per cent	20,312	13,542
Total net estate passing on death		£141,273

This shows an increase of over 41½ per cent on the present position.

From the fifth to the seventh year the value of the gifts for duty purposes will reduce in accordance with the following scale:

5th year	85 per cent
6th year	70 per cent
7th year	40 per cent

The sums assured by the gift protection policies will decrease in the same proportions but the reductions may have the effect of reducing the total dutiable estate so that a lower percentage of duty is charged on the free estate.

At the end of seven years the gifts will no longer be dutiable and duty will only be chargeable on the free estate as follows:

Total free estate	£33,854
Estate duty at 21 per cent	7,109
Net estate passing on death	£26,745

Also, as the children will have received a gift of £150,000 less the gift protection premium, the true amount passing has risen to:

Net value of gift	£127,731
Net value of free estate	26,745
Total	£154,476

This is an increase of 54 per cent over the present position. In addition, the husband and his wife have a guaranteed income for the rest of their lives as shown below.

2. Income

During the joint lifetimes of husband and wife they will enjoy an income from the annuity which will continue during the life of the survivor.

The free estate will also yield an income but as a large part of this is likely to comprise the house and personal effects it is assumed that the gross income is only 2½ per cent per annum overall.

It will be noted that a large part of the income from the annuities is free of tax. This tax free part will remain unchanged throughout the joint lifetimes and will increase slightly if the wife dies first but reduce a little if the husband predeceases her. This does not affect the gross income which remains constant throughout.

Return on free estate at 2½ per cent (see above)		£846	0s	0d
Income content of annuities		2,850	0	0
Total taxable income		£3,696	0s	0d
Income tax	£1,349			
Surtax	213	£1554	0s	0d
Net taxable income		£2,142	0s	0d
Add capital content of annuities		3,822	0	0
Total net spendable income		£5,964	0s	0d

An increase on the present position of 39 per cent.

Income of widow

If the husband dies first and, after payment of duty, the free estate no longer produces income, the widow would nevertheless have a guaranteed income for her lifetime of:

Income content of annuity		£3,138
Income tax	£1,366	
Surtax	137	£1,503
Net taxable income		£1,635
Add capital content of annuity		3,534
Net spendable income		£5,169

Note: This contrasts very favourably with the position if the plan had not been effected when she would probably only have an income of 5 per cent of the original net estate, i.e.

£100,000 at 5 per cent	£5,000
Less income tax and surtax	2,440
Net spendable income	£2,560

PLAN XXXIII

It is assumed that a man aged 45 next birthday has an earned income of £4,000 a year. His assets consist of house and contents worth about £20,000 and Stock Exchange securities valued at £30,000, making £50,000 in all. The present estate duty liability on this is £15,500.

The purpose of this plan is to accumulate a tax free fund which can be drawn upon to pay the duty arising on death. The plan takes advantage of the fact that Clause 37 of Finance Act, 1968, allows exemption from estate duty of gifts which were part of the deceased's 'normal expenditure'. Accordingly a whole life policy is written under the Married Women's Property Act for wife and children, the whole of the proceeds of which (since the premiums can be expected to be well within the normal expenditure limits), will be available free of charge to pay the duty on the rest of the estate. But, of course, in a period of inflation the estate is likely to increase considerably in value as the years go by. It is logical in these circumstances to choose a policy the value of which is likely to respond to similar inflationary trends. This would be an equity-linked whole life in preference to a traditional with-profits policy, since the value of the latter is not directly determined by the market price of equities from time to time. In other words the equity-linked policy achieves a closer matching of assets to liabilities *at any particular point in time.*

EQUITY-LINKED WHOLE LIFE ASSURANCE

Guaranteed sum assured payable on death	£15,500
The amount payable on death is the value at the bid price at that time of units deemed to have been purchased to that date (less an allowance for the company's liability for tax on any capital gains) *Plus* that part (if any) of the guaranteed sum assured which has not been deemed to have been applied in the purchase of units	

Annual premium(s)	£319 2s 0d
Income tax saving	52 13 0
Net annual cost	£266 9s 0d

Note: The maximum number of years' premiums payable (n) will be 85 minus age next birthday at inception. When the policy(s) is effected and in each subsequent year until a year's premiums have been paid $1/n$th of the basic sum assured is deemed to be applied to purchase units at the offer price then current less a discount of $1\frac{1}{4}$ per cent.

Estimated Claim Value

Assuming the units increase in value at the rate of 5 per cent per annum, the amount payable in the event of death will be:

If death occurs after	10 years	£19,142
	15 years	£21,452
	20 years	£24,180
	25 years	£27,450
	30 years	£31,341
	35 years	£36,022
	40 years	£41,617

If the value of the units dropped at the end of say two years the amount payable would be the guaranteed sum assured of £15,500.

Surrender Values and Paid-up Benefits

The policy illustrated acquires a cash surrender value after two years' premiums have been paid. After three years' premiums have been paid the policy may be converted into a paid-up assurance free from payment of future premiums. On conversion, the benefit payable on death will be the cash value at the bid price of units deemed to have been purchased to date subject to deduction in respect of tax on any capital gains provided that the benefit will not be less than the total amount deemed to have been applied in purchase of units.

ESTATE DUTY FUNDING: ALTERNATIVE METHOD

Where the estate is substantial and the premiums required outside 'normal expenditure', it is advantageous to make gifts out of capital which are applied by the beneficiaries as premiums to a similar policy on the life of the estate owner. In this way, the charge for duty is diverted to the premiums payable in the last seven years before death, the proceeds of the policy itself remaining exempt.

Part Four

GENERAL

21

Policy Conditions

THE NORMAL procedure for obtaining life assurance is to complete a proposal form, which is then considered by the insurance underwriter in the light of the information given in it and a doctor's report. If he is satisfied with this information, the company will then issue a letter of acceptance. The letter of acceptance constitutes an agreement on the part of the company to insure the life proposed on the terms stated on payment of the first premium within a specified period, normally 30 days, and subject to no change of health within these 'days of grace'. On payment of this premium a contract of life assurance exists, and it is normal for the company to assume risk at the same time. It is important to remember that the policy, which is issued afterwards, is not a contract. It is a written document providing evidence of the contract that has already been made. The Stamp Act, 1891, imposes a penalty on a life assurance company which fails to execute a duly stamped policy within one month of receiving or taking credit for a premium, which makes a policy a legal necessity.

There is very little statutory regulation of the form or conditions of life assurance policies and, in practice, they vary widely. But most up-to-date companies, in the interests of speed and economy, use standard printed documents, with a framed space, called the schedule, for filling in detailed particulars. A schedule policy commonly covers the following points in the order given:

(1) Name and address of the company, policy number and sometimes salient particulars of the policy, e.g., sum assured, premium, due dates, term of assurance. With the exception of the policy number, these particulars are unnecessary as they are repeated in the schedule. This

part of the document usually bears the insurance company's crest.

(2) Recital that the contract is based on a proposal, particulars of which are given in the schedule.

(3) Statement of the contract. This commonly commences with a recital that the first premium has been paid and goes on to say that if subsequent premiums are paid as provided in the schedule the company will, upon proof of the happening described in the schedule and the title of the claimant, pay the sum assured. Sometimes, this recital is extended to include conditions for establishing claims, e.g., proof of title must be presented to the company's chief office where settlement will be made.

(4) Schedule of particulars including any special conditions peculiar to the contract. The headings might be as shown on page 179.

(5) General conditions and regulations. These are important to the extent that one part of them limits the scope of the assurance and another part extends its benefits. The former are by custom called 'conditions' and the latter 'privileges'. Conditions and privileges differ considerably between companies and, in certain circumstances, may be sufficiently important to influence the choice of a particular contract. For this reason they are dealt with in some detail below.

Restrictive Conditions

These concern moral or physical hazards which the company is unable or unwilling to cover, at least at its normal rates.

Suicide.—It is still usual to state that the assurance is void in the event of suicide occurring within a specified period (e.g., two years), although interests of third parties may be protected and discretion exercised in favour of dependants. Many companies, however, refuse to accept that a person will take out life assurance with the express object of taking his own life, or that life assurance could tempt him to do so, and so leave out this condition, although they may have second thoughts if the amount of

	Policy No.:	(With or Without Participation in Profits)
	Name and Residence of Proposer:	
	Name and Residence of Life Assured:	
	Age taken as:	Whether age admitted or not:
	Date of the Proposal and Declaration	
Sum Assured	Amount:	
	Event on which payable:	
	To whom payable:	
Premiums	First Premium:	
	Renewal Premiums and how Payable:	
	Premiums and Benefits Payable:	
	Special Provisions (if any)	

assurance is unreasonable in relation to the person's circumstances. For example, a labourer who asked for an assurance of £20,000 might (even today) arouse suspicions.

Occupation.—Over the last few decades there has been such an improvement in working conditions, housing and social services, that occupation is no longer an important underwriting consideration. Accordingly, only old-fashioned companies make much of this and it is usually wiser to ignore them anyway. But there are certain jobs which obviously involve special hazards, e.g., divers, jockeys, racing drivers, professional boxers, steeplejacks, etc. Publicans have also proved to be a heavy extra risk. All these occupations may be rated up from, say, 5*s* to £1 per cent. Workers in atomic plants and in factories where radio-isotopes are used may possibly be exposed to extra hazards, but mortality statistics do not reveal this at the moment. It is not now usual to charge extra for normal flying as a fare-paying passenger on recognized air routes, but special premiums may be charged for pilots and aircrew.

Foreign residence and travel.—The restrictions at one time imposed almost universally on foreign residence and travel are now rapidly disappearing. A clause may now be inserted in a policy if, at the time of the proposal, there is an immediate intention to live in certain areas which lie outside the temperate regions.

Where these restrictions are imposed, the policy normally provides that the assurance shall be void if the assured travels beyond these limits, unless the company's permission has been obtained and any required extra premium paid. But in an age when more and more people are regularly travelling round the world on business, restrictive clauses on travel are thoroughly old-fashioned. Most good companies now issue policies which, as a matter of course, are world-wide and unrestricted. No enterprising business man should normally accept any other.

Privileges

The wording of a policy provides for the payment of the sum assured on condition that all premiums are paid as they fall due. The clauses considered below are those which relax this general condition and provide for modified benefits in the event of discontinuance. Without these privilege clauses, failure to pay the premium on the due date given in the policy might result in immediate forfeiture of all benefits. This could operate very harshly on the policyholder, since part of the premiums he has paid in the early years of the assurance are more than sufficient to meet the current risk and have been put into reserve. If premiums are discontinued, this reserve will be surplus to the company's requirements and normal considerations of equity suggest that it should be released in some form. Naturally, the first call on this reserve is to maintain the benefits in the event of a temporary delay in payment of premiums. In fact, there are three distinct periods during which the benefits are to some extent preserved.

(1) *Days of grace*
The first period is that of the days of grace. This is normally worded 'thirty days of grace are allowed for the payment of renewal premium'. Normal practice is to accept the premium at any time within these days without any charge for interest or other penalty.

(2) *Non-forfeiture*
The non-forfeiture period immediately follows the days of grace. If a claim occurs during this period, the sum assured is payable subject to deduction of all premiums in arrear plus interest. Sometimes a fee is charged as well. A natural corollary of this is that the full benefits can be reinstated during this period on payment of what would otherwise be deducted without medical evidence.

The exact terms of this privilege vary widely between companies. In its most liberal form it provides that renewal premiums shall be automatically advanced to the policyholder as loans against the security of the policy, and that this procedure shall be continued until the total premiums advanced, and interest, exhaust the surrender value of the policy. In effect, therefore, the surrender value is used to pay the premiums plus interest as and when they become due, and if a claim arises during this period the sum assured is payable, less the total amount so applied. If the policy shares in profits, the cash value of bonuses accruing during this time will help to prolong the period during which the policy can be kept in force. The privilege may, however, take a more restricted form. For example, some companies impose a time limit irrespective of the amount of the surrender value. This could be one year only, after which the policy lapses. Any surrender value remaining is then held at the disposal of the policyholder.

It is worth mentioning that an unlimited non-forfeiture provision can, in certain circumstances, prove a disadvantage. It places the onus on the policyholder to surrender or make the policy paid-up if this is his intention, as it normally would be in the case of a policy kept up for the benefit of another if that other person died (e.g., a policy effected by a husband under the provisions of the Married Women's Property Act for the absolute benefit of his wife).

The following are examples of these two types of non-forfeiture provision:

'Unlimited' non-forfeiture

(*a*) If any premium is not paid within the days of grace and if no application for a paid-up policy has been made, then:

(*i*) if the surrender value of this policy exceeds the premium then overdue and any other unpaid premiums or other indebtedness to the company with interest thereon calculated up to the next renewal date, this policy will remain in force throughout the period up to the next renewal date:

but

(*ii*) if the surrender value does not exceed the premium then overdue and any other unpaid premiums or other indebtedness to the company with interest thereon calculated up to the next renewal date, this policy will remain in force only for such equitable portion of the period up to the next renewal date as may be determined by the company and will then lapse:

(*iii*) if this policy has no surrender value it will lapse.

(*b*) Any premium not paid within the days of grace shall form a first charge upon this policy, carrying compound interest as from the due date at such rate as the company may from time to time determine, provided that if the interest payable would amount to less than 5*s*, a fee of 5*s* shall be payable in lieu thereof. Any such unpaid premiums with interest may be paid at any time whilst this policy continues in force.

'Limited' non-forfeiture

Notwithstanding that a policy has lapsed by non-payment of a premium or instalment of premium the company will, on the happening of the event in which the sum assured becomes payable, pay the sum assured under the policy, subject to deduction of all arrears of premium with interest thereon at a rate not less than 6 per cent per annum subject to the following conditions:

(*i*) The said event occurs within 12 calendar months of the due date of the first unpaid premium or instalment of premium.

(*ii*) The net surrender value of the policy (after deducting any charge or lien which the company may have on the policy, together with any interest accrued thereon) calculated as at the end of the said period of twelve months on the footing that all premiums then in arrear have been paid, is of an amount not less than one year's premium.

A policy which satisfied condition (*ii*) of this provision, and which has not been reinstated within the said period of 12 months, will, at the expiration of that period, be automatically reinstated as a paid-up assurance for a reduced sum assured free from payment of further premiums, unless the amount of such paid-up assurance would be less than £50.

(*c*) *Conditional revival*

The third period during which some measure of benefit is preserved to the policyholder is normally applied to a policy which has not acquired a surrender value and enables the policyholder to restore the assurance on payment of arrears of premium plus interest, subject to satisfactory medical evidence. The advantage of this provision is that it is both cheaper and more convenient to carry on with the same policy than to start all over again with a fresh one, whilst only the minimum medical evidence may be required.

Example of revival clause
'If this policy lapse through non-payment of a premium it may be revived at any time within a year from the date of lapse provided that all overdue premiums and interest thereon (or, at the company's option, a fee of five shillings in lieu of interest) are paid and satisfactory proof is produced without expense to the company of the continued eligibility for assurance of the life assured (and of the child, if one be mentioned in the Schedule).'

Surrender Values and Paid-up Policies
Most policies contain special clauses about surrender and paid-up values. These expressions cause a lot of difficulty and in view of their importance, e.g., when it is desired to borrow against the security of a policy or to discontinue it, they are worth studying closely.

A surrender value is a feature peculiar to life assurance. It arises because the risk of death, which increases with age, is met by an annual premium which does not increase. The balance of premium not required to support the risk in the early years of the assurance is, therefore, put into reserve and accumulated to meet the liability arising in the future. The existence of this reserve enables the company to refund a portion of the premiums paid in past years if the policy is cancelled. The amount it is prepared to refund at any time is called the surrender value. In practice, the surrender value is always less than the premium reserve, for three main reasons. First, it is assumed (though not always correctly) that many of those who withdraw from the contract are in above average health, and to this extent disturb the balance of the mortality assumptions with possible adverse effect on the life fund. Secondly, withdrawals add to expenses, especially when they are matched by a corresponding influx of fresh proposals. Thirdly, the company expects to make a profit and looks to surrender values as one of its sources. Apart from the importance individual companies attach to these points, the amount of surrender value will, of course, also be influenced by investment considerations.

Again, practice differs widely amongst companies on the amount of information they include in the clause dealing with surrender values. Some conditions merely state the number of premiums that must be paid before a surrender value can be claimed. This may be anything from one to three years. Other companies give a basis on which the minimum surrender value will be based, such as 40 per cent of all premiums paid, exclusive of those paid in the first year, plus, in the case of a with-profits policy, the cash value of all bonus additions. The basis described is a minimum and may be well below the amount the company is prepared to allow in practice, especially if the policy has been in force for some years. The reason for this is that a schedule policy is used for many different types of policy, and for some, only a small surrender value can be allowed. For example, a whole life policy with unlimited premiums will have a much lower surrender value than a short-term endowment policy under which a much greater proportion of the premium in the early years is being put into reserve. However, a few companies do write into the policy the surrender values (or minimum surrender values) applicable at each stage of the contract, and this can be extremely useful in enabling the assured to assess the market value of his policy at any time. With this information, he knows always how much he can borrow against the security of the policy and can plan accordingly if the need for borrowing arises.

However generous a company might wish to be on the matter of surrender values it has always to take account of its responsibilities to those policyholders who continue. Whether surrender values should be guaranteed or not, and what scales should apply, are questions which involve investment policy. Life assurance is essentially a long-term proposition and the results achieved depend to a significant extent on long-term investment. If a company were to be over-generous in the surrender values it allowed, it would invite heavy calls on its funds and have to prepare for these by investing a correspondingly greater proportion of its funds in short-dated securities yielding lower rates of interest. A company may, therefore, quite legitimately seek to discourage surrenders in the best interests of its policyholders in general.

An alternative to surrending a policy is to have it made paid-up for a reduced sum assured. The reduced sum assured is payable instead of the full sum assured at the time the policy matures, i.e., at death, if the policy is whole life, and at death or at the end of the specified period, if endowment. In the case of an endowment policy and a whole life policy with limited premiums, it is normal practice to allow a paid-up policy for a sum assured which bears the same proportion to the original sum assured as the number of years' premiums paid bears to the number originally payable. This is called a fully proportionate paid-up policy. Thus, if a 15-year endowment policy were taken out for a sum assured of £1,500, the paid-up sum assured after three years' premiums had been paid would be three-fifteenths of £1,500, namely, £300, payable at the end of the period or at previous death. Most people naturally feel that this gives them their rightful share in the policy, based on what they have paid, although theoretically the proportionate basis may be wrong. In the case of a whole life policy with premiums payable until death, the paid-up sum assured would be calculated by converting the surrender value into a reversionary amount.

A point of importance about paid-up policies is whether and at what time they will continue to participate in profits. Here again, practice differs between companies. Some will allow a paid-up policy to participate after, say, two or three years' premiums have been paid. Others will convert the paid-up sum assured calculated on the proportionate basis to a higher amount, with no future participation. Where this last practice is adopted, a higher than average surrender value may be granted and this may prove the more attractive alternative.

Loans

Almost all companies are prepared to grant loans on their policies, at a rate of interest which normally does not exceed bank rate, up to nearly the full amount of the surrender value. Sometimes the policy will contain a clause which states that a loan will be granted up to an appropriate percentage, say 90 per cent, of the surrender value. The rate of interest will not normally be mentioned. Nor are the terms of repayment usually referred to, but normally the loan can be repaid at any time, or can be allowed to remain as a permanent charge on the policy, provided that premiums and loan interest are promptly paid. How valuable the privilege can be is illustrated in Chapter 13, which deals with the provision of school fees on a basis which allows the cost to be spread over as long a period as possible with the help of loans from the company against the security of an endowment with-profits policy maturing at the end of the fee-paying period.

22

Medical Underwriting

IF LIFE assurance were compulsory for everyone there would be no need for medical tests, for premiums could then be based on mortality statistics derived from a study of the entire population. The premiums would be too high for some, too low for others, but on average the profits and losses would balance out. As, fortunately, life assurance is not universally dispensed in this way, it is necessary for companies to impose tests so that they avoid being saddled with a preponderance of people whose health is below average and who are, naturally, the most interested in life assurance. The purpose of the medical tests is then to sort out this class so that they may be dealt with separately. In this way, the life fund can be kept in balance and the business of insurance carried on rationally.

The need for selection having been established, what sort of medical tests are necessary? The ideal test is, of course, a doctor's examination. One might suppose that the majority of people would welcome the opportunity of undergoing a medical examination free of cost to themselves, but apparently this is not so. At best, it is considered a nuisance. At worst, some people fear a medical examination so much that they will forgo life assurance altogether rather than submit to it. These objections are reinforced by the knowledge that the company will not reveal the details of the examination to them; so that if the report is adverse, the proposer is left with his private speculations. (The chief medical officer of the company, however, will, as a rule, be prepared to disclose details to the applicant's own doctor.) As a result, companies are now prepared, within limits, to make the initial selection themselves, by means of a carefully devised questionnaire. A good deal of thought has been given to this. On the one hand, there is a natural desire that the proposal form in which the questions appear be kept as simple as possible. On the other hand, there must be enough information for the underwriter to form a correct assessment of the risk. If the company considers the answers to these questions are satisfactory, that may be as far as it needs to go; or it may wish to make further enquiries of the proposer's own doctor. This method of selection without medical examination is generally available today for people under the age of 45–50, where the sum to be assured does not exceed £5,000. A few companies currently go up to £10,000 for whole life and endowment assurance, and higher limits are frequently available for temporary assurances or family income benefits. In all other cases, or where any real doubt remains in the underwriter's mind, a medical examination will be called for.

Medical Examination

The medical examination may be arranged with the company's own doctor at its head office, or with a local doctor. Each company keeps a list of doctors throughout the country with whom these examinations can be arranged. Most people usually prefer to be examined by their own doctor but this is discouraged by companies in order that they may, if necessary, obtain a second opinion on any adverse feature, and also to avoid possible friction between doctor and patient. Most companies, however, are willing to allow women to be examined by their own doctors.

The doctor is given a detailed questionnaire which he answers, partly from questions put to the proposer and partly from his own observations. He is then asked briefly to summarize the results of his examination, and to place the proposer in one of a number of defined categories. The following classification is typical:

Class I Good lives, who may be accepted at normal rates of premium.
Class II Below average lives, where personal or family history or present condition justify an extra premium or other special terms.
Class III Non-insurable lives.

More information may then be required for Class II.

Life Assurance without Medical Examination

The proposal here is, of course, more comprehensive than the form used where a medical examination follows automatically. Normally, a full statement of family and medical history is required and the answers are made the subject of a warranty, but the information required by individual companies varies. A few consider family history sufficiently unimportant to omit it altogether; some require answers to questions about specific diseases; others are content to ask a general question or questions about the proposer's state of health without reference to particular impairments. The upper age limit for non-medical acceptance is usually 50, sometimes 45 for whole life and 50 for endowment assurance, and the maximum sum assured that will be considered without medical examination varies amongst companies from £2,000 to £10,000 or more. Naturally, the insurance company reserves the right to ask for a medical examination if it feels this is necessary after considering a proposal on this basis.

What the Insurance Underwriter Looks Out For

The premium rates used by insurance companies for life assurance are based on mortality investigations carried out among males accepted for whole life and endowment assurance at ordinary rates of premium. The mortality table commonly used today is based on experience during the four years 1949–52. As well as present health, medical or family history and personal habits are what normally interest the underwriter, and if these compare badly with the average for the class of people investigated and the difference is at all marked, then the risk of mortality is likely to be greater than the premiums allow for and special terms may have to be imposed. It is outside the scope of this book to deal with the relative importance the underwriter is likely to attach to the very wide variety of physical impairments which he has to consider, but of special interest to him is the relationship between the proposer's weight or bodily measurements and his height. Life assurance is a very empirical business and experience clearly shows that fat people, on average, do not live as long as thin people. So when an applicant for life assurance is medically examined the doctor records height, weight, the measurements of the chest when he has breathed in and out, and also his waist. From these measurements he decides whether his subject is big-boned and muscular, or just fat. If he decides he is fat, he will be on his guard for any sign of high blood-pressure or impairment of the heart. It is interesting to note that, since weight in relation to height is apparently higher in the average American than in the average Briton, it is likely that American or American-owned insurance companies take a more lenient view of overweight for life assurance.

Below-average Lives

These are the people who do not manage to get into the first class, but are accepted into the second. They are insurable but are considered to give rise to an additional risk and this is covered in one of the following four ways:

(1) *Extra premium*
This may be assessed by adding so many years to the applicant's age, but more commonly now by applying a percentage of the sum assured to the normal premium for his age. In the first case, whatever the class of assurance, the extra premium is assessed from the whole life table of rates. Thus, if a person aged 25 next birthday wanted to take out an endowment assurance and was rated up five years, the additional premium charged would be the difference between the whole life premium at the age of 25 and the whole life premium at the age of 30, about 4*s* 6*d* per cent. If the extra risk is likely to reduce in the future, the additional premium may be imposed for only part of the period of the assurance.

(2) *Fixed debt*
In this case, the sum assured is subject to a reduction if a claim arises within a fixed period of years. Where a policy is being taken out primarily for investment purposes, this is likely to be preferable to payment of an extra premium.

(3) *Diminishing debt*
Under this system, which is now used wherever possible instead of the fixed debt, the debt against the sum assured decreases by level amounts each year until it finally disappears. Unfortunately, this reduces cover initially by a larger amount than if the debt were fixed, which might be the reverse of what is desired. It is the present practice of the Inland Revenue to ignore the debt in assessing the 7 per cent limitation for tax relief.

(4) *Change of policy*
If the extra risk is likely to arise at a much later stage, it may be possible for the company to offer instead of a whole life, an endowment assurance, or even a whole life assurance with limited premiums.

Sharing the Risk

An interesting plan recently introduced by one enterprising company for under-average lives provides for the payment of an extra premium which is returned in full if the insured survives the period of the assurance. Naturally, the extra is more than would be charged under a standard policy, but with the certainty of a full return on survival. The plan should, therefore, appeal to the person who rates his chances of survival reasonably high and is prepared to back his own judgment in the matter.

The following example illustrates the possible advantages:

Proposer—aged 30 next birthday assessed as 'below-average' risk.
Policy—£5,000 endowment assurance without profits maturing at age 65.

'*Standard Policy*'

Normal annual premium	£91
Additional annual premium to cover 'below-average' assessment, say	25
Total annual premium	£116
Amount payable on death or at age 65	£5,000

'Special Policy'

Normal annual premium	£91
Additional annual premium to cover 'below-average' assessment, say	33
Total annual premium	£124
Amount payable on death or at age 65	£5,000
Plus: on survival an amount equal to all the additional premiums (35 × £33)	1,155
Total amount payable on survival at age 65	£6,155

Pooling for Below-average Lives

One of the chief difficulties in dealing with people who are not average in the special sense explained above is the lack of sufficiently detailed statistical information on which suitable rates can be assessed. The insurance underwriter usually has only medical evidence on which to work. Below certain accepted standards, any proposer is classified as a 'below-average' life. Although there are many shades of 'below-average', underwriters are governed by the statistics available and cannot afford to be optimistic. In an attempt to get a better idea of certain risks one re-insurance company is now operating three pools, covering diabetics, people suffering from high blood-pressure, and people suffering from coronary diseases.

Diabetics

All classes of policy can be considered up to £20,000.

High blood-pressure

This was started in 1953 to provide cover for people whose high blood-pressure was not attributable to any known cause. Again, all types of policy can be considered up to £20,000.

Coronary disease

The same now applies, although when the pool was first started in 1957 the class of policy was originally restricted to endowment assurances, decreasing temporary assurance and income benefits payable up to the age of 70 and for not more than 20 years. The experience has, therefore, been in this case relatively favourable. Preliminary results are now being studied which should make possible a better assessment of the risks attaching to these conditions. Companies participating in the pool automatically re-assure with each other an agreed proportion of the risks.

Specialist Re-assurance Market for Below-average Lives

Whilst this pooling system operates through normal company channels, it is limited in its scope. In general, the best prospects for below-average lives lie with the specialist re-insurance market with its extensive international links. This is only accessible through brokers. The re-insurers may underwrite the whole of the risk element and use one of a number of direct companies chosen by the broker to issue the policy. People of below-average health are well advised to consult a broker, who is often able to place their life assurance on more favourable terms by dealing with the matter in this way.

23

How They Invest Your Money

LIFE ASSURANCE companies exist to pay benefits when they fall due. But the size of these benefits, the value for money they represent, depends to a large degree on the skill with which the companies manage the savings entrusted to their care. It is natural, therefore, that present and potential life assurance savers should want to know something about the way in which companies invest their premiums, since this is one fact to be taken into account in judging the merit of this form of saving as compared to others.

The first point to make clear is that companies enjoy complete freedom to invest new money coming into their hands, and to switch existing assets in whatever way they judge best. And this explains the wide differences in the results they achieve under their with-profit policies. For although, as a group, they share the same responsibilities and face problems of a similar type, there is wide scope for differences of opinion and judgment as to the best way to use this freedom. The second point, which is commonly taken for granted though without a full appreciation of its implications, is that over and above all other considerations stands the responsibility of a company to provide complete security. Under the terms of its policy, a company undertakes to pay the sums assured on the happening of the events insured against, or at the end of the period specified, and it is irrevocably committed to this monetary guarantee. Its position is, therefore, totally different from that of, say, a unit trust, where the risk of capital loss is borne by the investor.

A life assurance company, then, must have money of the right amount available at the right time. If this were the sum total of its concern, the investment and valuation of its fund would not present any undue difficulty by modern actuarial standards. It could minimize one element of risk by investing wholly in fixed-interest stocks and, to a large extent, match the term of its assets to the period of its liabilities. But it is a fair bet nowadays that merely to conserve money and earn for safe keeping a modest return will partially defeat its own object. In an era of persistent currency inflation, the average investor demands more cover, for he is concerned with protecting the *real* value of his savings.

Life assurance companies have not been slow to recognize this and to adjust their investment policy to changing economic conditions in order to produce better results for their policy-holders. Experience over many years has shown that a well-spread portfolio of equity shares yields a steadily rising income. Closely connected with this is the rise in the value of the shares, which is a reflection of this favourable experience projected into the future. Over the same period (allowing for some fluctuations) there has been a continuing rise in the market rate of interest, and a corresponding fall in the value of fixed-interest securities. These features of the post-war investment market were appreciated by a number of companies at an early stage and have influenced to a greater or lesser extent all companies in the way they have since invested new money coming into their hands. This is demonstrated in Table 1 below, which traces the pattern of gilt-edged and equity investment over the last nineteen years.

This table, and the other which follows, is compiled from figures supplied by the British Insurance Association, based on returns supplied to the Association by member companies. The British Insurance Association's members transact 80 per cent of the home and overseas business of the British insurance market. It will be seen that, from 10½ per cent in 1947, the stake in equities rose to 22½ per cent of the total assets at the end of 1961, and the same pattern is repeated in property, which has strong equity features. The stake in property has however continued to increase, to 11½ per cent at the end of 1967, whereas the equity stake has stabilized itself and there is some reduction.

However the proportions of equity shares shown in Table 1 are based on book values, which in most cases are well below market values. *If ordinary shares were written up to current market values in the balance sheets, the proportion of total assets in equities would be considerably higher.* This difference between book and market values provides most companies at the present time with substantial hidden reserves, which are likely to enable them to meet

TABLE 1

DISTRIBUTION OF LIFE AND ANNUITY ASSETS

Year	*Fixed interest stocks (per cent)*	*Ordinary shares (per cent)*	*Property (per cent)*
*1947	83·6	10·6	5·8
1957	73·0	17·6	9·4
1958	71·4	18·9	9·7
1959	69·4	20·6	10·0
1960	68·0	21·9	10·1
1961	67·0	22·4	10·6
1962	67·4	22·0	10·6
1963	67·3	22·1	10·6
1964	67·1	22·5	10·4
1965	67·3	22·0	10·7
1966	67·2	21·5	11·3
1967	67·6	20·8	11·6

* Including non-life assets.

depreciation in ordinary shares on a much larger scale than is ever likely to be encountered in time of peace. From the point of view of with-profit policyholders, these reserves give strong backing to the present high level of bonuses.

The table indicates a general trend. Individually, however, companies have reacted in widely different degrees to the attractions of equity and property investment. As regards equities, for example, at the end of 1963 there were at least three companies with less than 15 per cent of total life assets (at book values) in ordinary shares. At the other end of the scale, a few companies held approximately one-half of their assets in this form.

Table 2 breaks down the current position in greater detail and shows the average percentage of assets invested in the various classes of security at the end of 1967. Once again it must be pointed out that variations about the average are considerable amongst the companies represented.

TABLE 2

DISTRIBUTION OF LIFE AND ANNUITY ASSETS 1967*

	Class of investment	*Percentage of invested assets*
1	Mortgages	17·9
2	British Government and British Government guaranteed securities	18·3
3	Commonwealth Government Provincial and Municipal Stocks	2·2
4	Foreign Government Provincial and Municipal Stocks	0·9
5	Debentures, loan stocks, preference and guaranteed stocks and shares	21·7
6	Ordinary stocks and shares	20·8
7	Real property and ground rents	11·6
8	Other investments	6·6
		100·0

* Figures just released for 1968 show little change.

The present life and annuity funds and the corresponding assets as shown in these two tables reflect the liabilities of life assurance companies for payment of benefits *in the future*. At the end of 1967, these funds stood at over £10,000 millions, representing an increase of over 100 per cent over the previous decade. The investment income of these funds was some £690 millions and the income from premiums approximately £1,330 millions. As against this, payments to policyholders in respect of claims by death and maturity, gross annuity payments and surrenders totalled about £750 millions. Thus the funds are more than replenished by premiums and investment income as current claims are met, so making it possible for companies which continue to expand in this way to extend the term of their investments in certain classes of security, if a higher yield can thereby be obtained, at the same time leaving good equity investments undisturbed.

What of the future? First, the short-term outlook. The Finance Act, 1965, which introduced capital gains tax affects the investment of life funds chiefly in two ways. First there is the capital gains tax which is chargeable on the profits *realized* by the sale of securities in the life and ordinary annuity funds. Of course, life funds have for decades been taxed on their *actual* capital profits in respect of their annuity funds. But the taxation of realized capital gains on life funds is new, and the starting point is the price of stocks as they were at 6th April 1965.

In the past, where money has been invested in gilt-edged stocks, very active switching has taken place because the life fund was subject to tax only in respect of its interest earnings. Following the introduction of capital gains tax it looked as it the difficulties involved in switching would make gilt-edged less attractive. Whilst different considerations apply to different insurance companies it does not look as if these difficulties have had much effect on the proportion of gilt-edged stock taken up. With some insurance companies, debentures have been the favourite fixed interest stock in the past because they have given a higher yield than gilt-edged, with satisfactory security. We have recently seen a very high return (9 per cent) on debentures but these compete for favour as much with equities as with gilt-edged stock. This is because, although the yield is less, gilt-edged are more marketable than debentures and hence more attractive to very active funds which have decided to carry on with switching much as before. There is no evidence that insurance companies are willing to allocate more money to mortgages, which remain unattractive as an investment for well-managed funds, although they may be attractive for other reasons in providing an extra source of non-profit business.

On the equity side capital gains tax has less immediate importance as life assurance companies tend to regard equities as a long-term proposition providing a source of rising income rather than one of capital profit. This statement, however, needs some qualification because if an insurance company invests in equities yielding 3¼ per cent rather than debentures yielding 9 per cent it must pay out capital appreciation in part or penalize unfairly one generation of policyholders. And as indicated in Chapter 2, the changing pattern of bonus distributions under with-profit policies indicates that an increasing portion of capital profit is being brought into the distributable surplus.

The 1965 Finance Act also, of course, changed the whole taxation basis of companies. The uncertainty about future rates of corporation tax immediately affects insurance companies in their capacity as investors to the extent that it makes it even more difficult for them to assess, within an acceptable margin of error, the future income available to shareholders, and thus the proper value of the shares. Partly for this reason and partly because of the high return obtainable at the present time on fixed-interest stocks the proportion of insurance company assets invested in equities is unlikely to be increased in the near future, although of course the market value of these has increased rapidly over the last few years. One or two insurance companies have given details of the improvement which has taken place and an indication of the addition this makes to their reserves.

Taking the long-term view however the fortunes of equities must be closely linked with the fortunes of our economy as a whole. If our economy continues to expand then it is reasonable to hold that the income from the equity portfolio of life funds will continue to rise as well. New forms of taxation and the very high differential between fixed interests and equity yields may arrest this progress at times, such as at present, but in the long run it should be maintained.

The traditional reversionary bonus system was based on the ability of life office actuaries to anticipate to a large degree the sources of future profit and to dispose of it smoothly. Equities create difficult problems in this respect as, where they represent a substantial part of the underlying investments, it becomes necessary under this system to assume some future rate of growth so that a progressive part of the improvement in value of these shares can be brought into the surplus from which normal bonuses are paid. This can only be done up to a certain point, beyond which special bonuses have to be added and it seems likely that the latter will become a permanent feature of traditional policies in the future, thereby reducing the gap between these and equity-linked contracts.

In general, the outlook for policyholders is promising on two counts. First, because normal life policies are not subject to capital gains tax when they become claims by death or maturity. Secondly, because the improvement in the capital value of these policies largely arises from earnings on securities held supplemented by appreciation in their market values as distinct from profit on sale. This does not, of course, mean that they are free of this tax at source, or that the incidence of capital gains tax calls for a passive investment policy (quite the opposite today), but that the realization of profits on which tax is due is not forced upon the companies and is, to a large extent, within their own control.

24

The Role of the Broker

It is an axiom that life assurance is sold and not bought. In other words, the initiative lies with the seller. Unfortunately, in this country, almost anyone is free to sell insurance whether he knows anything about the subject or not. Thus solicitors, accountants, bank managers, estate agents, commercial travellers and a host of others can acquire agencies with various life assurance companies which enable them to earn insurance commissions as a profitable sideline. Whilst many companies *claim* to be strict in the standards they require of their agents, the facts belie this. Against this confusing background there is all the more need to understand the services provided by a life assurance broker. Anyone who is interested in life assurance would be wise to consult a broker before taking out a policy. It normally costs nothing to do so, but may save a considerable amount of both time and money.

One must, however, begin by asking what a life assurance broker is, since he has no clearly defined professional status which distinguishes him from commission agents in general. (Other than membership of the Corporation of Insurance Brokers, which now has a special life assurance division, entitling those who by examination or otherwise qualify to call themselves 'Incorporated Life Assurance Brokers'.) It is simplest to answer this by examining a broker's responsibilities to his client, and these will be considered under the following:

(1) Selecting the company.
(2) Arranging the policy to achieve the best financial result.
(3) Servicing the policy after completion.

Selecting the Company

A representative selling life assurance will naturally emphasize the advantages of the policies issued by the company he represents.

If he acts responsibly, he will also point out any disadvantages of a particular policy, to avoid any misunderstanding which might give rise to dissatisfaction later. The representatives employed by good companies normally act with a high degree of responsibility in this matter, but it is no part of the representative's job to invite his 'prospect' to consider the alternative contracts offered by other companies in competition with his own.

There are, in fact, over one hundred companies transacting life assurance in this country at the present time, and nearly every year a few new names are added. As a group, these companies do not offer uniform rates of premium and bonuses. On the contrary, remarkable variations occur in the values of their policies. It is a broker's responsibility to assess these values and to make appropriate recommendations to his client. In a nutshell, *the broker does the shopping for him.*

In making his selection, a broker seeks the best terms that can be obtained from a company of good repute. He normally makes no charge for this service as he is remunerated by the company with whom he places the business. It follows that an essential qualification for a broker is that he is an appointed agent of all companies transacting life assurance, so that he is fully conversant with their policies and is able to select freely amongst them. There are, however, a very few companies which do not pay commission, although they may pay for reasonable expenses incurred in placing business with them. A broker will not necessarily ignore these companies but, if the occasion arises when he recommends one of them, he may have to request a fee from his client. It is an admitted weakness in a system which otherwise guarantees the broker's complete independence.

These are the main points to which a broker may need to give his attention before recommending a particular company:

(*i*) *Rates of premium*

If the policy is a non-profit type, say, whole life offering a fixed sum on death, it is possible for the broker to demonstrate exactly how much each company wants by way of annual premium for a specified sum, or, conversely, what sum is offered for the same annual premiums of a defined number. At this, the simplest level, quite large differences emerge. For example, a run through current published rates of *leading* companies shows that a man aged 30, seeking a policy to secure £3,000 on his death with premiums limited to age 65, may find the cost varying from £41 15*s* 0*d* to £54 a year, a difference of £428 15*s* 0*d* in the total paid. Put another way, one-fifth of the gross premiums paid to the wrong company would have been wasted.

(*ii*) *Bonuses*

With-profit policies are much harder to compare, because the sum to be paid at the end of the day is not known. It is certainly not enough to take the basic sums assured secured by a given premium and compare the estimated amounts payable at maturity if current bonus rates are maintained. For one thing, bonus changes do not occur smoothly but in steps when declarations are made; allowance must therefore be made for those companies whose last declarations have left them temporarily behind their competitors but who may overtake them at the next valuation. Allowance must also be made for the fact that some companies tend to be more conservative than others in the rates they declare and carry larger reserves. In other words, if bonuses are regarded as dividends, some are better covered than others and there may be more to come. An example of this is the payment of special bonuses from reserves. The broker will look at all these things in relation to the term of the policy, but will make his final assessment from his own knowledge of the quality of their investment management, on which bonuses ultimately depend.

Much may depend on selecting the right company when the policy participates in profits. A recent survey, which covered only a small proportion of the life assurance companies operating today, showed that over a 50-year period with premiums of £25 a year, the differences between one company and another can be a sum representing the cost of over 76 per cent of the annual premiums. An interesting point arising from this and other surveys carried out over shorter periods is the fact that some companies consistently show relatively bad results; so much so that, if all life assurance was placed through brokers, they would have to do much better or close down.

(*iii*) *Medical underwriting*

The standards of medical selection call for careful consideration in cases where some doubt exists about health, or weight is above average. The standards vary amongst companies and it is clearly of no avail for a broker to base his selection on the company quoting the best rate for a healthy life if his client is not likely to be placed in this category by the company of his choice. Some companies are lenient in their requirements for acceptance at normal terms, others more stringent; some companies take a particularly strict view of certain medical conditions, whilst others are more ready to acknowledge the progress made by medicine in correcting these. The broker will use his judgment in border-line cases to decide how far rates should take second place to the probability of a good underwriting decision.

Where ill-health obviously excludes the possibility of first-class acceptance, the broker may prefer to deal with the matter outside normal company channels and through re-insurers who underwrite the risk. He would then select one of a number of companies with whom arrangements with the re-insurers apply, to act as a front company and produce the policy.

(*iv*) *Paid-up and surrender values*

The terms allowed by companies on discontinuance show wide variations. The representative of a company will naturally not wish to dwell on the least favourable outcome of the policy he sells, but it is a broker's responsibility to see that his client is left under no misapprehension which may cause dissatisfaction later. Sometimes, the plan put forward allows for complete or partial discontinuance at a later date and in these cases paid-up and surrender terms naturally assume greater importance.

(*v*) *Other policy conditions*
Policy conditions are now generally subject to fewer restrictions than in the past but, where any restrictions apply, the broker will wish to see that the terms are as far as possible fixed at the outset and not subject to adjustment if the circumstances of his client change later. This applies particularly to the question of foreign travel and residence. Non-forfeiture provisions, and facilities for borrowing which may not be covered in the policy document, may also call for attention.

(*vi*) *Efficiency*
The general standards of efficiency and helpfulness of a company are very important and the broker is well placed to compare one company with another in the light of his own experience. A broker may be able to speed up decisions and cut through a certain amount of red tape, but ultimately he depends on the efficient management of the company to spare his client unnecessary delay and inconvenience. Those companies which make it their practice to give quick and helpful service from the time they receive a proposal until the day the proceeds of the policy are paid out will obviously receive special consideration.

Achieving the Best Financial Result

It has been assumed so far that selection is being exercised by the broker within *a given class of assurance*. Sometimes, however, the exact insurance provisions required are not clear at the beginning. There may be a number of possible alternatives, the results of which have to be worked out and compared before the correct answer emerges.

The responsibility of the broker to achieve the best financial result is considered here in relation to those circumstances where the choice of the type of assurance and the disposition of the benefits have important financial consequences in terms of tax and estate duty. Since all life assurance has financial consequences of this kind, tax and estate duty considerations can never be ignored, but a broker is frequently approached for advice where the problem of saving tax is paramount and life assurance is sought primarily as a means of securing this saving.

It might be thought that questions of tax are more within the province of the professional accountant and that the broker would confine himself to recommending the insurance policies only. In practice, however, both solicitors and accountants very frequently turn to brokers for assistance in formulating suitable plans to mitigate the effects of tax and estate duty. A broker is uniquely placed to give informed advice because he has not only his own specialist knowledge to draw upon but also the much larger pool of intelligence provided by all the companies with whom he does business. There is not likely to be any problem capable of satisfactory solution by life assurance to which someone in one of the insurance companies does not know the answer, and if the broker cannot solve it himself he generally knows where to look for assistance. Brokers sometimes originate new policies or schemes which are adopted by companies but, far more often, they sift and utilize the best of the material the companies put forward.

When a broker draws up a plan for, say, mitigating estate duty, he will usually work in close collaboration with his client's solicitor and/or accountant. This is desirable, because a great deal of background information may be needed and life assurance may form only part of a wider scheme that is being put forward. Apart from this, the broker, although he may have lawyers on his staff, cannot accept responsibility for legal advice as such.

Servicing

The relationship between a good broker and his client continues after a policy has been arranged. Changes in the policyholder's circumstances are likely to require additions to, or modifications of, the original assurance. By keeping in touch with the policyholder, the broker is able to ensure that the original plan continues to fulfil his needs. If the policy has been effected direct with a company or through an agent other than a broker, this contact is unlikely to be maintained. A company is certainly not bound to watch over future developments and advise its policyholders when it is no longer suitable to keep certain policies in force, nor is it organized to do so. A broker, on the other hand, has a special interest in seeing that those he has advised continue to be satisfied, for this is the best way of ensuring that they return to him. Brokers do not have a 'public', such as a nationally-advertised name attracts, and therefore rely to a large extent on the support of existing clients and their friends.

Servicing is not confined to recommending modifications or additions to existing policies. In many cases, the need for further help after a policy has been completed first arises when a loan is required on the security of the policy. It may arise again over the exercise of a conversion option, or the need to revise the terms of a policy for estate duty or other reasons. The policyholder may require advice on the application of non-forfeiture provisions, if he has not been able to retain his premiums. If he failed to secure his assurance at normal rates of premium in the first instance, there may be scope for negotiating improved terms later if his health has improved. The most important of the occasions requiring the broker's intervention is when the policy matures for payment. Whether this is by death or survival, the broker who arranged the policy has a responsibility, which he shares with the company, to see that, the conditions of the assurance having been fulfilled, the proceeds are paid promptly and that they reach their intended destination.

Responsibilities to the Company

Whilst a broker's first duty is to seek the best terms he can for his client, he must judge what is fair to the other side, too. There are likely to be many occasions when a broker can persuade a company to relax its normal rules in a policyholder's favour by establishing a reasonable case, which may be based on the practice of the company's competitors. There are other times when, even if the company might be persuaded to meet the policyholder's wishes, it could be wrong for the broker to push persuasion so far. Life companies hold public money on trust, they have a duty to see that insurance is properly administered and if, as a result of extreme pressure, they yield to unreasonable demands, this is bound to create unfairness or inefficiency.

Other Considerations

Life assurance used to offer considerable scope for tax avoidance on a large scale. By transferring capital to life policies huge amounts of estate duty and surtax could be saved. Since the Finance Act, 1968, the scope for tax avoidance has been dramatically reduced but opportunities still remain through policies of life assurance to circumvent the 'intentions' of the law, though the action required now involves more complicated transactions than were previously necessary. These opportunities leave the broker who is sufficiently expert to appreciate them in a continuing difficulty over the possible conflict of interest between his duty to his client and his social obligations. Many people, though not the beneficiaries of such transactions, dismiss the distinction between tax avoidance and tax evasion as a mere quibble, but the distinction is well understood by those trained in the law. In the author's view, however, the conflict is not one of a moral or social nature, since in our legal system the intentions of the law are inferred from its letter and, mercifully, legal decisions are not, as they might otherwise be, dependent on subjective judgments. Strictly speaking, therefore, it is not possible in matters of this kind to circumvent the intentions of the law if you stick to its letter. On the other hand, if loopholes are actively exploited this might prove harmful to the long-term interests of life assurance. The repercussions of the 1968 Finance Act were less widespread than was feared; but the complexity of the provisions introduced is harmful in itself. In the long-term interests of life assurance, therefore, a broker shares with insurance companies a responsibility to use reasonable discretion in advising on the use of life assurance for tax avoidance and to refrain from promoting schemes which are likely to precipitate further anti-avoidance legislation.

Conclusion

Because life assurance brokers still have no fully recognized professional status it is the more difficult to choose between the good and the bad ones, bearing in mind that almost anyone with some knowledge of life assurance can set himself up as a broker and be recognized as such by the majority of companies. Amongst broking firms there will be those who deal in general insurance as well, which is a different branch calling for quite separate skills. The fact that a broker covers both general and life business does not in itself demonstrate weakness in the life branch, but it is reasonable to expect that life assurance should be the exclusive concern of certain people in the organization and, where this is so, it will normally be conducted in a separate department. In the case of many of the larger broking houses, e.g., at Lloyd's, separate departments for life and pensions have been maintained for upwards of 50 years and, since the last war, many of these have become established as separate companies in their own right. The sense of responsibility and service to the client characteristic of Lloyd's brokers is normally a continuing tradition in these subsidiary companies. There are, however, many good life assurance brokers outside the Lloyd's tradition.

Part Five

FOR THE EMPLOYER

In this final part, life assurance and associated benefits are dealt with on a group basis. The schemes outlined are designed for the employer and can be successfully integrated with provisions made for staff superannuation.

Pensions are, of course, the most important of the provisions an employer can make for his staff with the help of life office underwriting and administration, and in the best-run companies they form part of wages and salaries policy. This is a subject of particular interest to the author, but one so big and so varied in its insurance and non-insurance aspects that it falls outside the scope of this book. In the case of small schemes, however, the benefits are often funded by setting up endowment insurance policies on lines similar to those described for individuals in Chapter 17.

25

Group Insurance

Voluntary Life Insurance

Introduction

THE IDEA behind this type of scheme is to enable employees to pay premiums on life assurance policies in the easiest way possible —by weekly or monthly deductions from their pay—on specially favourable terms. The employer does not contribute, except indirectly by taking over the job of premium collection and remittance. An employer can do this with relatively little trouble through his salary and wages department, but from the insurance company's point of view the opportunity to collect premiums in bulk is so economical that it can afford to offer terms at least as good as those applicable where premiums are paid annually in advance.

The essential feature then of the scheme is that the premiums are collected in instalments by deduction from pay and remitted in bulk by the employer to the insurance company at agreed monthly or quarterly intervals, in arrears. The scheme is on an entirely voluntary basis. The employee alone decides whether he will join and what size of policy he takes out. The employer, for his part, decides whether the scheme should be open to all employees or only to those in particular grades. He will normally prefer to confine it to this permanent staff who are less likely to leave.

Voluntary life assurance schemes are of two kinds: restricted schemes and comprehensive schemes.

Restricted Schemes

These are schemes in which only a particular kind of policy can be taken, usually endowment assurance with or without profits. The employee is, however, entirely free to decide how large a policy to take out at any time, according to the amount of premium he wishes to pay. This type of scheme is the more popular of the two, especially where voluntary life assurance has been introduced in conjunction with a pension scheme as a means of supplementing the pension benefits. The uniformity of the benefits simplifies the procedure for effecting policies and it is usually possible to obtain from the insurance company more favourable rates and conditions than those available under a comprehensive scheme. Another point in favour of a restricted scheme is that it is clearly easier, where choice is restricted to one company, to select a company which is competitive at all ages for one class of policy than for, say, half a dozen.

Comprehensive Schemes

In these schemes, the employee is free to choose any policy he likes within the range offered by the insurance company. The comprehensive scheme was pioneered by one insurance company as far back as 1859 and it has operated this type of scheme continuously ever since. A comprehensive scheme offers the more valuable welfare facility, but it is necessary to exercise some care in selecting which policies are worth taking out under the scheme and which are better dealt with in the open market.

To derive the full benefit from a comprehensive scheme, employees must be given the opportunity to explain their circumstances to someone who can advise them as to the kind of policy best suited to their needs. There may be someone in the company with the necessary experience to give this guidance, and where the employer has a reliable person available for this purpose it is probably the best arrangement of all. If the employer does not have a suitable person on his staff, it is important to ensure that the insurance company, or broker, is able and willing to provide the services needed. Certain times should be set aside when those interested in taking out policies can be interviewed. It also helps if a representative of the broker or the insurance company can be allowed to give a talk on life assurance, say, once a year, to new employees.

Advantages of the Scheme

The chief advantage to the employee of a voluntary life assurance scheme is that it gives him the opportunity to assure his life at no more, and sometimes less, expense than if he were paying premiums annually in advance, although he will actually pay them in a way which is far more convenient. In addition, there will usually be other advantages dependent on the particular terms offered by the insurance company. Some insurance companies, for example, are willing to give improved surrender values and to accept a very simple proposal form, with only two or three questions about health, for sums assured up to, say, £2,500. Normally, full cover is given immediately a proposal is accepted. On the other hand, it is important to recognize the scheme's limitations. It is essentially designed for small policies where the advantages of the scheme in terms of simplicity and convenience outweigh the savings at certain ages and for certain classes of policy that might be obtained from other insurance companies. Where larger policies are required, it is advisable that a broker be consulted, and, for this reason, where a broker has placed this type of scheme, there is usually an arrangement between him and the insurance company for any enquiry or proposal for assurance above an agreed figure to be referred to him, so that he can consider whether it should be placed elsewhere. In this way, the employer can feel assured that the interests of his employees are fully safeguarded and that they have an opportunity of securing the best terms available.

From the employer's point of view, the scheme gives him an opportunity to add to the welfare arrangements he has made for his staff. As the premiums that have been collected are remitted to the insurance company in arrear, the employer is never called upon to finance the scheme by remitting premiums before they have been collected. There is thus no cost to him beyond the administrative work of deducting premiums and accounting for them.

EXAMPLE

The following is an example of a restricted scheme in the form in which it might be addressed to staff.

(1) *Eligible employees*
Any employee, male or female, may join, provided they are permanent employees.

(2) *Contributions*
Your contribution must be in units of 1*s* a week and must be large enough to produce a minimum sum assured of £100, ignoring bonuses, but in any case a contribution cannot be less than 3*s* a week.

(3) *Benefits*
The amount of your assurance depends on the age at which you start to contribute, and on bonuses allotted in future years. It becomes payable when you reach the maturity date, which is the policy anniversary prior to your sixty-fifth or sixtieth birthday, whichever is your normal retirement age. Should you die before the maturity date, the sum assured, together with any bonuses attaching, would be paid to your estate. The benefits are free of income tax. Alternatively, the sum assured, together with bonuses, may be utilized to purchase an annuity to supplement your pension. The policy will contain a guaranteed annuity rate.

(4) *Method of collecting contributions*
Contributions will be deducted from salary or wages and, once terminated, can normally only be re-started for a new policy and subject to satisfactory completion of an application form.

(5) *Cessation of contributions*
If contributions are terminated before the maturity date, a cash surrender value will be payable. The amount of this repayment under the policies illustrated will be at least one-half of the contributions paid (if no bonuses have been surrendered). Alternatively, the benefits secured by past contributions may be left to your credit

as a proportionate paid-up policy to be paid at maturity date or earlier death.

(6) *Temporary absence*

If your contributions fall into arrear by reason of temporary absence, and the policy has not lapsed during such absence, the arrears of contributions must normally be made up in one payment or by double deduction for a period. Should the arrears be for more than 13 weeks, however, some other alternative may be necessary and in such a case the company would arrange direct with you some adjustment of the policy benefits.

(7) *Leaving service*

If you leave the service of your employer before the maturity date for any reason you will have the following options:

(*i*) You may keep the policy in force by continuing your contributions direct to the insurance company (for the smaller policies quarterly or half-yearly premiums will be required). Monthly premiums will be accepted if paid by banker's order.

(*ii*) The policy can be made 'paid-up', i.e., by ceasing contributions and leaving the policy with the insurance company until the maturity date, when a proportionately reduced sum assured would be paid.

If the policy were to be made 'paid-up', it would continue to participate in profits in respect of the reduced sum assured and existing bonuses, provided three full years' premiums had been paid. Under this option, no monetary loss would be suffered by a contributor.

(*iii*) You may discontinue the policy altogether and take a cash surrender value. Under the Voluntary Assurance Scheme, an extremely favourable guaranteed minimum surrender value of 50 per cent of the premiums paid is granted from outset under the policies illustrated, whereas under a normal policy a surrender value is not granted until two or three years have elapsed, and then is only a small proportion of premiums paid.

(8) *Rebate of income tax*
Your contributions to the Voluntary Assurance Scheme are treated for tax purposes as ordinary life assurance premiums and not as expenses.

(9) *Policy*
Each contributor will be issued with a separate policy and have all the rights possessed by the individual policy-holder.

(10) *Enrolment*
The benefits shown in the schedule are for with-profit endowment assurances maturing in the sixty-fifth and the sixtieth year of age, but should you wish to vary these terms then suitable arrangements can usually be made with the insurance company on application.
If you wish to contribute to this scheme, will you please complete the enclosed special application form?
If the answers are satisfactory, no further information will be requested, provided the cash benefit is less than £2,500.
Policies may be effected on the first day of any month.

Note: It is possible to arrange this type of scheme with equity-linked policies as well, subject to a higher minimum contribution.

Group Life Assurance

Introduction

A group life assurance scheme gives the employer an opportunity to cover his staff against death in service at a lower cost than they would have to bear individually to secure equivalent protection. Not only does the insurance company offer favourable term assurance rates of premium but, by taking a group of lives on a non-selective basis, it can usually afford to dispense with medical evidence for part or all of the cover required. It is thus possible to provide within the framework of this type of scheme life assurance cover for people who, as individuals, might be uninsurable or insurable only on adverse terms. The insurance company can offer life assurance free of medical evidence only so long as it is dealing with all employees in a definite category or categories, thus eliminating the risk of underwriting an abnormal proportion of below-average lives.

This type of scheme is very commonly linked to a pension scheme but is available on its own to any employer who has a sufficient number of eligible personnel.

The Basis of the Scheme

A group term assurance policy is issued to the employer and provides for the payment of a capital sum on the death in service of the employees admitted to the scheme. The amount of benefit can be uniform for each member, or it can vary according to wage or salary scale, length of service or grade of employment, in accordance with the employer's requirements. The policy is renewable yearly.

The operation of the scheme is governed by a simple set of rules which define the categories of employee included under the policy, when an employee is eligible for cover, the amount and type of benefit and the procedure for meeting claims.

EXAMPLE

The following is a summary of the terms and conditions offered by one company which has made a speciality of this type of scheme.

Evidence of Health

Provided an employee is actively at work on the date he enters the scheme, no evidence of health is required unless his death benefit exceeds either £10,000 or 10 per cent of the total sum assured under the group policy. Eligible employees absent (provided continuous absence does not exceed 2½ years) on account of illness on the entry date will be covered automatically where the group consists of 200 or more—otherwise after two months' continuous service on returning to work.

Unrestricted Cover

The policy provides unrestricted cover, including civil war risks and overseas residence. Service risks are also covered provided premiums are continued for the employees concerned.

The standard rates of premium normally apply, irrespective of the nature of the employer's business or of the nationality of employee.

Employee's Option on Leaving Service

An employee who leaves the service of the employer, either prior to, or on normal retirement at, or before the sixty-fifth birthday, has the option to effect a whole life or endowment assurance, without evidence of health, at a premium rate applicable to the age attained. This option is available for a sum assured up to the amount for which the employee was covered under the group scheme at ordinary terms at the time of leaving.

Administration

The administration of the scheme is very simple—both at inception and on renewal. Where the total number of employees is 200 or more, a statement by the employer of the total number to be covered, together with a breakdown of ages into four broad age groups, is all that is required initially and at five-yearly intervals. If the benefit is related to salary, a certified declaration of the total salary roll of each age group is necessary.

At each anniversary date of the scheme during each five-year period, a statement of the total number to be covered in the ensuing year (or the total salary roll if applicable) is all the information the insurance company needs to calculate each renewal premium. An adjustment is made on the basis of the latest data to allow for any variation in the average total benefits insured during the previous year.

For groups of under 200, the names and dates of birth of each employee are required—together with details of salary or wages, if appropriate.

Premiums

Provided the group consists of 50 or more employees the company offers a flat-rate premium guaranteed for five years, for each £100 of benefit. This method of rating not only eases administration but enables the employer accurately to assess future costs, within the period of guarantee, in relation to total membership and benefits.

For groups of under 50 employees, scale premiums are used.

Scale premiums applicable to groups of under 50 lives. To provide a capital sum of £100 on the death in service of any insured employee, the scale premiums for one year's cover are as follows:

Age next birthday of employee	*Scale premium per £100*
Up to the age of 40	4*s*
41 to 55	10*s*
56 to 60	20*s*
61 to 65	40*s*

The company guarantees that the scale premiums will not be increased for original members of a group—either in respect of the renewal of initial benefits or increases in benefit resulting from salary increments. Three months' notice is given of any revision of these rates which may apply to new entrants.

Flat rate applicable to groups of 50 or more lives. A premium rate is calculated according to the distribution of ages and cover in each of the above age groups. The average rate for a group of lives is usually under 10*s* per annum for each £100 of benefit. The gross cost of providing a death benefit equal to one year's salary or wages is, therefore, only about one-half per cent of the pay roll.

The rate applicable at the inception of a scheme is guaranteed for a period of five years.

Profit Sharing

Where the number of employees is 200 or more, and the sum

assured is not less than £200,000, it is possible to have a profit-sharing arrangement, subject to an addition of 10 per cent to the normal annual premium. The employer would then be entitled to 75 per cent of any sum remaining after deducting all claims paid or notified during the year of insurance from 80 per cent of the premiums for that year. Negative amounts would not be carried forward.

Widows' and Orphans' Scheme

Introduction

The benefits provided under group life assurance schemes are seldom adequate for married men with families. To cover fully the needs of a widow with, say, two children to support, the capital sum payable on death might have to be increased to as much as five years' salary. Instead of providing such large capital benefits, some employers prefer to see that the widows of employees who die in service are assured of a permanent income. A widows' and orphans' pension scheme is one way of solving the problem where it is desired that the benefits should be fully guaranteed by an insurance company and not paid from an existing superannuation fund to which additional contributions have been applied for this purpose. In considering the provision of widows' pensions, however, the long-term effects of inflation must be remembered. A lump sum benefit of equivalent present value, if wisely invested, will offer to a young widow more real protection than a fixed income for the rest of her life, on which the insurance company may stand to make a very substantial profit. In the author's view, therefore, this type of scheme, unless it is practicable for the employer to adjust the benefit in course of payment, should not be substituted for group life assurance but may be usefully added to it.

EXAMPLE

The scheme outlined below provides assistance, (a) *for a widow until she dies or remarries,* (b) *for children should the widow die prematurely and (c) for the children of widowers, up to a maximum of £300 a year. This is, of course, only an example of such a scheme and, in practice, the benefits and eligibility would be adjusted to suit the individual requirements of the employer.*

Eligibility

The scheme will be open to new entrants on the commencement date and on each subsequent anniversary, these dates being referred to as 'entry dates'.

Employees will be included in the scheme on the first entry date when they are within the following category:

> Full-time married male employees, ordinarily employed in Great Britain and Northern Ireland, who are aged not less than 21 and not more than 64 years, other than those whose employment is of a temporary or casual nature.
>
> *Note:* The expression 'married male employees' also includes a widower with a child under the age of 21, or a divorcee having the legal custody of a child under the age of 21.

The employee will be responsible for notifying the company of his marriage.

If an employee is absent from work owing to injury or illness on the day when he first becomes eligible, he will not be entitled to the benefit of the scheme. He will become entitled to this benefit on the day on which he completed two months' continuous active service after return to work (except as qualified below).

No evidence of health will be required from present or future employees, provided a sufficient percentage of those eligible join the scheme at its commencement, and so long as the total number of employees assured under the scheme does not fall below a specified minimum, except that evidence of health may be required before a member's benefits may exceed certain limits.

By permission of the company, and subject to any requirements of the insurance company, arrangements may be made in special circumstances for the inclusion of an employee who does not completely satisfy all the qualifications of eligibility.

Benefits of the Scheme

In the event of the death of a member while in the service of the company and prior to his sixty-fifth birthday, the annual pension (as set out in Table 3) will immediately become payable by monthly instalments in accordance with the following provisions:

(*i*) If the member leaves a surviving widow the instalments will be payable to her until her death or earlier re-marriage, except as provided in (*ii*) below;

(*ii*) if there is a surviving child or children of the member under the age of 21,

(*a*) at the date of the widow's death without her having remarried,

or

(*b*) at the date of the member's death if he was a widower or divorcee,

the instalments of pension will be payable to the company in trust for the benefit of the child or children and will be payable for so long as there is a surviving child under the age of 21.

The company will, at its discretion have absolute power to apply the whole or any part of the instalments of pension which may be paid to them as described above for the advancement, maintenance or benefit of the child or children in any manner which they may think fit, and may accumulate and invest on behalf of the child or children any surplus not so applied.

Note: The terms 'child' and 'children' include step-children and legally-adopted children of the last marriage of the member, but do not include such children of any previous marriage.

Temporary Absence

If a member is temporarily away from employment, the company may maintain his benefit for a period not exceeding 2½ years if due to injury or illness, or 12 months if due to any other cause. If, at the expiry of this period, the member has not returned to work, his assurance under the scheme will be terminated. He will, however, have the right to exercise the 'Leaving Service Option' mentioned below.

Leaving Service Option

Subject to certain conditions, a member who, prior to his sixtieth birthday, has left the service of the company and ceased to be entitled to the benefit of the scheme, will have the right, upon written notice to the insurance company within 31 days after such termination, to obtain without medical examination an individual policy for a whole life or endowment assurance as then issued by the insurance company for individual lives, for an amount not exceeding 15 times the rate of annual pension applicable to his salary class at the time he leaves service. The rate of premium for such policy will be that then in use by the insurance company for his attained age, and the policy will be subject to such terms and conditions as assurances of the class selected are then granted to the general public.

Amendment or Discontinuance of Scheme

The company will have the right to amend or discontinue the scheme at any time.

Income Tax

Benefits under the scheme will be subject to deduction of income tax at the appropriate rate.

Estate Duty

Under the present practice of the Estate Duty Office, benefits arising under the scheme will be free of estate duty.

Certificates

Each member of the scheme will be given a certificate stating that his name has been recorded as a member of the scheme.

Non-assignability

Benefits payable under the scheme cannot be commuted and,

being strictly personal, cannot be assigned, charged or alienated in any manner whatsoever.

Notes:

(1) Members will be asked to produce birth certificates on joining the scheme. Otherwise, proof of age will be essential when the benefit becomes payable, and if the age of the member has been mis-stated, the benefit of the scheme will be adjusted by the insurance company. Proof of marital status will also be required when the benefit becomes payable.

(2) A member must notify the company on the occurrence of any of the following events:

- (*i*) in the case of a married member,
  - (*a*) on the death of his wife,
  - (*b*) on becoming a divorcee;
- (*ii*) in the case of a widower or divorcee,
  - (*a*) on the death of a child under 21 years of age if at that time there is no other child under 21,
  - (*b*) on the twenty-first birthday of the youngest child.

A member becoming a widower or a divorcee and not having a child under 21, or a widower or divorcee whose only child under 21 dies or whose youngest child reaches its twenty-first birthday, will cease to be a member on the last day of the month which day coincides with or follows the event.

TABLE OF BENEFITS

Salary class	*Annual salary*	*Annual pension payable by monthly instalments*
		(£)
A	Not exceeding £450	100
B	Over £450 to £550	125
C	„ £550 „ £650	150

Salary class	*Annual salary*			*Annual pension payable by monthly instalments*
				(£)
D	Over £650	to	£750	175
E	„ £750	„	£850	200
F	„ £850	„	£950	225
G	„ £950	„	£1,050	250
H	„ £1,050	„	£1,150	275
J	„ £1,150	„	£1,250	300
K	„ £1,250	„	£1,350	325
L	„ £1,350	„	£1,450	350
M	„ £1,450	„	£1,550	375
N	„ £1,550	„	£1,650	400
O	„ £1,650	„	£1,750	425
P	„ £1,750	„	£1,850	450
Q	„ £1,850	„	£1,950	475
R	„ £1,950			500

Note I. Changes of salary class take effect from the anniversary of the date of a member's entry into the scheme coincident with, or next following, the date of change in salary or wages.

Note II. 'Annual salary' means basic salary or wages only and does not include bonuses, commission, overtime or any other emoluments.

Group Sickness Insurance

Introduction

Rather more than half of the employed population are now covered by some form of sick-pay scheme. The majority of these arrangements only provide for payment of benefit for a limited period, which is often as short as 13 weeks. Thereafter, payment may be continued in certain cases at the discretion of the employer. It is normally best for the employer himself to finance limited arrangements of this type, because his liabilities are not excessive and the payments required are likely to be less than the premiums an insurance company has to charge to cover the relatively high cost of administering a large number of small claims. There is, however, a growing interest in the extension of sick pay to cover prolonged absence through illness or injury which may prove to be permanent. This is something which the average employer cannot contemplate providing without the help of insurance. By insuring the benefits, not only does the employer relieve himself of future worry, but in effect spreads the cost as evenly as possible.

At one time, the insurance market for this type of scheme was very limited and, because insurance underwriters lacked adequate claims experience, the premium they charged tended to be unreasonably high. Today, however, several schemes are available which make it possible for employers to cover their staffs for a generous level of benefits at a modest outlay.

Benefits in typical schemes are graded according to salary in a way which broadly takes account of National Insurance Sickness Benefit, with the provision that the scheme and State benefits do not exceed a reasonable percentage of earnings, normally 75 per cent. They are payable in the event of incapacity arising from sickness or accident, and this is generally interpreted as incapacity preventing normal attendance at work. Most companies withhold benefit if the claimant, though unable to follow his normal occupation, takes up alternative work, but one or two companies allow payment of benefit in this event on a proportionately reduced scale. It is normal in a group scheme for the commencement of payments to be deferred for a period ranging from four weeks to 12 months and to cease at normal retirement age, but not later than 65 in the case of men, and 60 in the case of women. If the employee was a member of his employer's superannuation fund, payment of a deferred pension can then be made, in addition to which he will receive his State pension.

Where there are many employees to be covered, the insurance company will normally issue a group policy. Where numbers are small, separate policies will be issued for each member of the scheme. The largest companies may prefer to finance their own scheme but re-insure very large benefits for their senior executives.

Income Tax Position

Subject to Inland Revenue approval, the employer's premiums qualify for relief as a trading expense. This relief extends to payments in respect of a controlling director only if the scheme also includes a reasonable proportion of staff and the controlling director's benefits are reasonable in relation to theirs. No tax relief is allowed on employees' contributions and for this and the other reasons mentioned below, schemes are normally wholly paid for by the employer.

The tax treatment of benefits depends on whether the employee receives them from the hands of the insurance company or from his employer. If they are received direct from the insurance company they are tax free until the employee has received them for a complete fiscal year. At the end of this period the benefits are taxable as unearned income. If they are received from the employer they are treated for tax purposes in the same way as payments of salary and are taxed in accordance with P.A.Y.E.

Employees earning over £2,000 a year, and directors, are liable to be assessed for income tax in respect of the employer's premiums if the scheme provides for payment by the insurance company direct to the employees. For this reason, it is usual to arrange for the benefit to be paid to the employer, who undertakes to pay an equivalent amount of salary to the employees, deducting tax as is usual for earned income.

Contributions by Employees

If employees are asked to contribute, any employee on the staff at the time the scheme is introduced would be free to refuse to join. If any of those who refused subsequently fell ill, the employer might be faced with an awkward decision. For example, if an employee had long service, his normal attitude prior to the scheme's introduction might have been to continue salary payments for a time beyond the date when benefits under the scheme would normally commence. Once the scheme had started, this might seem unfair to other employees who had been contributing to secure this benefit. Thus, where the employer is not prepared to provide full-scale benefits at his own expense, a better arrangement is a non-contributory scheme for a smaller benefit, coupled with provision for employees to supplement this by paying voluntary contributions to individual policies.

Alternatively, full-scale benefits can be given and the employees' share of the cost recovered indirectly by increasing their pension fund contributions by an appropriate amount.

EXAMPLE

The employer decides to insure against the risk of a prolonged breakdown in health of senior people in the organization and to define this by reference to a minimum salary level of £2,500 per annum.

Qualification for Benefit

Benefit is payable during the continuance of disability, excluding an initial 'deferred period' of six months, and disability would be defined in the policy as inability on the part of the employee by reason of sickness or accident to perform any part of the duties of his employment with the company while not following any other occupation.

Amount of Benefit

The benefit to be insured under the scheme is two-thirds of salary with a maximum benefit of £7,500 in respect of any one member. The employer for his part would pay this amount to the member subject to the total of the scheme benefit and State benefit not exceeding three-quarters of salary.

When a claim is admitted benefit would be paid by monthly instalments in arrear after the expiry of the deferred period, with a proportionate final payment in respect of a period less than 1 month. The amount payable under the policy would be determined by reference to salary on the premium date prior to the commencement of disability.

Method of Payment of Benefit

When a claim is admitted the insurance company would make the appropriate payments to the company, and the company would then make similar payments to the member, subject to deduction of tax under P.A.Y.E. in the normal manner.

Termination of Benefit

Benefit will terminate as soon as 'disability' ceases but not later than attainment of age 65.

If 'disability' ceases, but the employee is not able to resume the full duties of his employment with the company, so that a reduced salary is paid, the insurance company would be prepared to consider granting a reduced benefit on an 'ex gratia' basis. If granted, this would be calculated as that proportion of the full benefit which the reduction in salary bears to his salary at the time disability began.

Cessation of Employment while entitled to Benefit

Even if a member of the scheme leaves service while entitled to benefit the payment of benefit continues so long as disability lasts, but not beyond attainment of age 65. If he is able to take up a new occupation a reduced benefit will be payable, calculated in the same way as the 'ex gratia' benefit described above.

Exclusions

No claim will be admitted in respect of sickness or accident which in the opinion of the insurance company is wilfully self-inflicted or caused or aggravated by intemperence, or by a drug or drugs administered otherwise than under the direction of a Registered Medical Practitioner. Nor can any benefit be paid for disability which is caused or aggravated by a criminal act on the part of the insured, or is caused by hostilities, whether war be declared or not. Recreational activities, including winter sports, would normally be included, but special consideration would be given to motor racing or other sports of an exceptionally hazardous nature.

Medical Evidence

Assuming about 35 members with a total salary roll of £120,000 no medical evidence would be required for the first £100 of monthly benefit in any individual case provided the employee has not been absent from work in the most recent period of 3 consecutive months and is actively at work on the date he becomes eligible for cover.

Cost

The initial cost is likely to work out at between $\frac{3}{4}$ per cent and $1\frac{1}{4}$ per cent of the payroll, depending on the age distribution of the membership and the relative salaries. Naturally where the benefit is concentrated amongst the most senior people in the organization, the average age of membership is likely to be high and this would be reflected in the higher percentage cost.

Group Medical Insurance

Treatment in a nursing-home or private accommodation in a hospital lies outside the scope of the National Health Service and costs are high. But private treatment offers important advantages. Delays are cut to a minimum and the patient is able to exercise freedom of choice of specialists and consultants. Another advantage of particular interest to the businessman is that, with a private room instead of a general ward, he is able to receive visitors with greater freedom and so maintain some contact with his business affairs.

Most people know that it is possible to subscribe to various plans which cover the subscriber for part or all of the costs of private treatment. It is not generally known, however, that very much better terms are available where subscribers can be dealt with on a group basis. An employer is in a particularly good position to promote group insurance for his own staff. Group insurance terms are available where there is a minimum of ten directors or staff included in the plan.

The plan may be introduced on a contributory or non-contributory basis. No tax relief is allowed on employees' contributions but the cost borne by the employer is eligible as a trade expense. The benefits payable, either for employees or their dependants, are not chargeable to the member for tax under Schedule E, except in the case of directors and employees earning over £2,000 per annum, who would be liable under Schedule E in respect of the premiums only.

In assessing the merits of a particular plan the two most important points to be considered are these:

(1) Is the plan administered sympathetically and with the minimum of red tape?

(2) Does the plan give the best possible value for money?

On the second point, the choice may depend on whether the employer wants the plan to be partly or wholly paid for by his staff, and whether dependants of employees as well as the employees themselves will be covered for benefit.

The group rebates offered by one well-known organization, which will serve as a guide to what is available at the present time, are shown on page 234.

An extension to the 'Unit Scheme' covers general practitioner services. There is no subscription rebate but, with a total or assisted group, the employer may elect to pay some or all of the subscriptions.

It will be seen that an optional group costs nothing except the relatively small administrative service the employer is asked to provide; this involves the collection of individual subscriptions and their remittance in bulk to the insurers. In return for this service, employees receive a substantial discount on normal rates. But, if desired, an associate company can act as Group Secretary for a small administrative charge.

The employer may prefer to share the cost on an equal footing with his key personnel. The actual cost to the employer, if he adopts an assisted group basis, should not be more than about one half per cent of salaries, excluding tax relief.

Where the employer decides to bear the whole of the cost himself, he obtains the best terms of all. The choice of a total group basis therefore enables him to give senior staff a valuable emolument at relatively small additional expense.

BENEFITS:

There are nine units of benefit for hospital and nursing-home charges and three for specialists' fees (the 'Unit Scheme'); in addition, an optional extension may be added to the Unit Scheme to provide for general practitioner services (the 'General Practitioner Scheme'). Typical schedules of benefits are set out on pages 237–8. The following are samples of the conditions that apply.

(1) The full range of benefits applies to each person included for cover (i.e., husband, wife and each dependent child).
(2) The annual overall maximum benefit is fixed so high that it is never likely to be reached.

EXAMPLE

Types of Staff Group

	Rebate allowed on unit scheme subscription (per cent)	*Proportion of unit scheme subscription payable*	
		By the company (per cent)	*By the employee (per cent)*
Total Group The company pays the subscriptions for the entire staff, or for all staff in certain grades selected by the company. With this type of Group, the company provides staff with a valuable emolument and has at the same time the satisfaction of knowing that it has made the best provision against the direct and indirect expenses of staff illness	$33\frac{1}{3}$	$66\frac{2}{3}$*	Nil
Assisted Group The company contributes not less than half the subscription of each employee who joins the Group. This type of Group is particularly attractive to those companies that wish to enable key young men and women to obtain protection at low cost	25	$37\frac{1}{2}$*	$37\frac{1}{2}$
Optional Group The company sponsors the Group but does not contribute towards the subscriptions	20	Nil	80

*Subscriptions paid by a company for any of its staff are normally allowable for tax purposes. The net cost to the company is thus appreciably reduced.

(3) The organization guarantees to renew a member's contract each year, regardless of his health record after joining, without restriction.

(4) Although a new member of the 'Unit Scheme' must be under the age of 65 and of the 'General Practitioner Scheme', under the age of 55, there is no upper age limit at which cover ceases.

(5) A newly-born child can be registered without evidence of health or other formality.

(6) Abnormal dental and eye treatment is eligible for benefit.

(7) Benefit is available whilst a subscriber is temporarily overseas on business or holiday. (Special terms apply to staff employed outside the United Kingdom.)

General

The following notes are generally applicable to all medical insurance plans.

Private Treatment

Basically, charges are for accommodation and for specialist services. The cost of accommodation varies in different types of hospital and in different rooms in nursing-homes. Specialist fees are arranged with the practitioner in each case; in most of the hospital pay-beds in England and Wales (but not in nursing-homes) the fees are regulated by statute. Whenever possible, therefore, an estimate of fees and charges should be obtained before treatment begins.

Unrecognized Treatment and Private Accommodation

The services covered are set out in the various tables published by the organization operating the plans. Claims are not, for example, admitted for costs incurred at unregistered nursing-homes, hydros or nature-care clinics. Fees charged by people who are not recognized specialists are similarly excluded.

Dental Treatment

Routine dentistry, e.g., fillings and extractions are not normally eligible for benefit. Benefit may, however, be claimed for certain treatment, e.g., orthodentics, operations on the jaw and special treatment necessitated by accidents.

National Health Service

If an insured person is admitted to a hospital general ward and treated without charge under the National Health Service, a special grant *may* be made towards expenses directly associated with the treatment of the illness.

Treatment Abroad

Benefit to the same extent as in the United Kingdom is normally available when an insured person is temporarily abroad on business or on holiday.

THE UNIT SCHEME BENEFITS (Individual and Group Subscribers)

Accommodation and nursing	Unit	28	35	42	49	56	63	70	77	84
	Up to	£ s d	£ s d	£ s d	£ s d	£ s d	£ s d	£ s d	£ s d	£ s d
A. Charges made by a hospital or a registered nursing-home for treatment of illness or injury	each week	28 0 0	35 0 0	42 0 0	49 0 0	56 0 0	63 0 0	70 0 0	77 0 0	84 0 0
	each year	364 0 0	455 0 0	546 0 0	637 0 0	728 0 0	819 0 0	910 0 0	1001 0 0	1092 0 0
B. Charges for full-time home nursing by qualified nurses	each week	14 0 0	17 10 0	21 0 0	24 10 0	28 0 0	31 10 0	35 0 0	38 10 0	42 0 0
	each year	182 0 0	227 10 0	273 0 0	318 10 0	364 0 0	409 10 0	455 0 0	500 10 0	546 0 0

Specialists' fees	Unit	1	2	3
	Up to	£ s d	£ s d	£ s d
C. Surgeon's and anaesthetist's fees for an operation, including aftercare, according to classification	each major operation	80 0 0	115 0 0	150 0 0
	each inter. operation	44 0 0	64 0 0	84 0 0
	each minor operation	22 0 0	32 0 0	42 0 0
D. Specialist physician's fee for regular attendance in a hospital or nursing home	each week	21 0 0	24 10 0	28 0 0
	each year	147 0 0	171 10 0	196 0 0
E. Specialist's fee for radiotherapy	each complete course	76 0 0	96 0 0	116 0 0
F. Specialist's fees for consultation, pathology, radiology and physiotherapy:				
(i) In-patient treatment, and out-patient treatment related to hospital or nursing-home in-patient treatment	full cost to a total of, each year	44 0 0	60 0 0	76 0 0
(ii) Out-patient treatment not related to hospital or nursing-home in-patient treatment	50% of cost to a total benefit of, each year	25 0 0	35 0 0	45 0 0

EXAMPLE OF SUBSCRIPTIONS

		Subscriber without dependants									Subscriber with 1 dependant									Subscriber with 2 or more dependants								
Age at Entry or Annual Renewal		18–29			30–49			50 and over*			18–29			30–49			50 and over*			18–29			30–49			50 and over*		
	Unit	£	s	d	£	s	d	£	s	d	£	s	d	£	s	d	£	s	d	£	s	d	£	s	d	£	s	d
Accommodation and nursing	**28**	3	14	0	5	6	0	6	2	0	5	11	0	7	19	0	9	3	0	6	16	0	9	14	0	11	3	0
	35	4	14	0	6	15	0	7	15	0	7	1	0	10	2	0	11	12	0	8	13	0	12	7	0	14	4	0
	42	5	16	0	8	7	0	9	12	0	8	15	0	12	10	0	14	7	0	10	14	0	15	6	0	17	12	0
	49	7	1	0	10	2	0	11	12	0	10	12	0	15	3	0	17	8	0	12	19	0	18	10	0	21	5	0
	56	8	8	0	12	0	0	13	16	0	12	12	0	18	0	0	20	14	0	15	8	0	22	0	0	25	6	0
	63	9	17	0	14	1	0	16	3	0	14	15	0	21	1	0	24	4	0	18	0	0	25	15	0	29	12	0
	70	11	7	0	16	5	0	18	14	0	17	1	0	24	7	0	28	0	0	20	17	0	29	16	0	34	5	0
	77	13	1	0	18	13	0	21	9	0	19	11	0	27	19	0	32	3	0	23	19	0	34	4	0	39	7	0
	84	14	17	0	21	5	0	24	9	0	22	6	0	31	17	0	36	13	0	27	5	0	38	19	0	44	16	0
	Unit																											
Specialists' fees	**1**	5	11	0	7	19	0	9	3	0	8	7	0	11	18	0	13	14	0	10	4	0	14	11	0	16	15	0
	2	8	7	0	11	18	0	13	14	0	12	10	0	17	17	0	20	11	0	15	5	0	21	16	0	25	1	0
	3	11	14	0	16	14	0	19	4	0	17	11	0	25	1	0	28	16	0	21	8	0	30	12	0	35	4	0

*When a registration includes a person aged 55 or over at the date of joining, the subscription is increased by 10 per cent.

The General Practitioner Scheme

(An optional extension available to Subscribers to the Unit Scheme)

Should I apply to join this Scheme as well as the Unit Scheme?

Only if your doctor has accepted you as a private patient; you should have a word with him first.

Can I defer joining this Scheme until a later date?

Yes, provided that you apply to join before you are 65.

The benefits under the General Practitioner Scheme have been designed to provide a Subscriber and his family with substantial help to offset the heavy expenses incurred as a result of a prolonged illness or a severe injury. By excluding from eligibility for benefit the average normal expenses likely to be incurred in every year, subscription rates are lower than would otherwise have been the case.

Benefits (Individual and Group Subscribers)

Benefit may be claimed for each person, as follows:

(*a*) *Attendances and visits*

Fees charged by a General Practitioner for surgery attendances or visits to the patient's home:

Each attendance or visit, up to:

Scale C £1 5*s* 0*d* Scale D £2 0*s* 0*d*

after excluding for:

Subscriber without dependants—first 4 attendances in every year.

Subscriber with 1 dependant—first 7 attendances in every year.

Subscriber with 2 or more dependants—first 9 attendances in every year.

(*b*) *Drugs and medicines*

75 per cent of the cost of drugs and medicines prescribed by a General Practitioner:

Each person, up to:

Scale C £80 Scale D £100

after excluding for:

Subscriber without dependants—first £5 of cost in every year.

Subscriber with 1 dependant—first £8 of cost in every year.
Subscriber with 2 or more dependants—first £10 of cost in every year.

(*c*) *Operations*

Fees charged by a General Practitioner for performing an operation requiring a local anaesthetic:
Each operation up to:
Scale C £8 8*s* 0*d* Scale D £12 12*s* 0*d*.

Subject to the limits set out above there is no overall maximum to the amount of benefit payable in any one year.

Subscriptions (*Individual and Group Subscribers*)

		Annual	Quarterly
For each person:	Scale C	£5 8*s* 0*d*	£1 8*s* 3*d*
	Scale D	£7 8*s* 0*d*	£1 18*s* 9*d*

The subscription for a person aged 55 or over at the date of joining the Scheme is increased by 10 per cent.

Addendum

Finance Bill, 1969

THIS BILL, introduced at the time the second edition of this book is going to press, appears to have no direct bearing on life assurance in this country. However, some of its provisions, e.g., on loan interest and estate duty have an indirect bearing on the benefits obtainable from life assurance in certain circumstances.

There will doubtless be substantial amendments in committee and once Parliament has an opportunity to examine the detailed working of the proposals contained in the Bill the Government may well decide to modify or drop some of them. The following summarizes some of these proposals as they affect life assurance plans:

1 *Loan Interest*

Interest paid after June 30th 1969 on short loans or after April 5th 1970 on debts incurred for a year or more on or before April 15th 1969 will in general no longer be allowed as a deduction from taxable income. The interest will however be taxable to a recipient and in certain circumstances the payer must deduct income tax at the standard rate from the interest payment and hand this over to the Inland Revenue. Interest will however be allowed for money borrowed to purchase an estate or interest in land or for improving or developing the land or buildings to the extent to which such interest does not exceed a reasonable commercial rate. This means that interest will continue to be allowed for tax relief on normal mortgages, but not re-mortgages or second mortgages. But if these proposals are enacted life assurance policyholders will no longer obtain tax relief on interest on loans taken on the security of their policies. Plans XV and XVI and Plan XXII would suffer as a result of legislation on these lines.

2 *Estate Duty on Settled Property*

The new provisions appear to affect two main classes of settlement: those where a beneficiary has a limited interest, other than an interest for his own lifetime; and discretionary trusts.

So far as limited interests are concerned, the general effect of the provisions is to change the basis of calculation from the value of the remaining income that the beneficiary may have expected to receive at the time of his death to a charge on the capital value of that part of the fund from which interest is derived.

Discretionary trusts are affected in that, on the death of any beneficiary who has received income from the trust at any time subsequent to April 15th 1963, provided that he has not ceased to be eligible to be a beneficiary more than seven years before his death, a charge to duty will be made on that portion of the total assets of the trust as are represented by his share of the total income of the trust over the whole period that he has been eligible to be a beneficiary. Any estate duty charge based on an interest which ceased or was disposed of more than four years before the death of the beneficiary will, however, be subject to the normal graduated reduction.

3 *Estate Duty Scale*

The starting point of the new scale is £10,000 instead of £5,000, thus relieving thousands of small estates from duty altogether. The rates of duty under the proposed new scale operate separately on each slice of an estate instead of uniformly on the whole of the value of the estate below the point at which the rate changes, thus eliminating the scandal of so called 'marginal relief' whereby 100 per cent of the top slice of an estate often went in duty.

The table below shows the proposed effective rate of duty on estates of various sizes.

Principal value of estate	*Effective rate of duty per cent*	*Principal value of estate*	*Effective rate of duty per cent*
£10,000	0	£100,000	47·1
£20,000	13·1	£150,000	53·1
£30,000	18·8	£200,000	57·3
£40,000	25·3	£300,000	61·5
£50,000	32·3	£500,000	66·9
£60,000	36·9	£750,000	71·3
£80,000	42·7	£1,000,000	74·7

Where the principal value is £2,057,500 and above the maximum rate operates at 80 per cent.

Index